Perfectionism in School

Perfectionism in School

When Achievement Is Not so Perfect

Kathryn L. Fletcher and
Kristie L. Speirs Neumeister

MP MOMENTUM PRESS
HEALTH

MOMENTUM PRESS, LLC, NEW YORK

First published in 2017 by
Momentum Press, LLC
222 East 46th Street, New York, NY 10017
www.momentumpress.net

ISBN-13: 978-1-60650-927-2 (paperback)
ISBN-13: 978-1-60650-928-9 (e-book)

Momentum Press Psychology Collection

Cover and interior design by Exeter Premedia Services Private Ltd., Chennai, India

First edition: 2017

10 9 8 7 6 5 4 3 2 1

Printed in the United States of America.

Abstract

Investigating the complex relationship between perfectionism and academic achievement, advanced students and researchers are introduced to different conceptualizations and measures of perfectionism in the opening chapter. Subsequent chapters of this book then provide an in-depth exploration of factors known to influence perfectionism such as parenting, attachment, and personality, as well as academic outcomes such as motivation, stress, burnout, anxiety, and procrastination. In each chapter, avenues for future research are highlighted to extend the exploration of perfectionism and academic achievement. In the final chapter, we have proposed a theoretical model for future work on perfectionism and academic achievement and have discussed additional areas that, while less well researched, deserve attention for their potential influence on how perfectionism may impact academic achievement.

Keywords

academic achievement, academic burnout, academic procrastination, academic stress, achievement motivation, attachment, parenting, perfectionism, personality, test anxiety

Contents

Preface

For the last six decades, the study of perfectionism has received considerable attention from professionals across disciplines including health, clinical psychology, sports psychology, and educational psychology. While their theoretical approaches and research methods may differ, experts across these different fields have shared the common goal of understanding the positive and negative consequences of perfectionism. What exactly is perfectionism? How do personality traits interact with environmental influences to develop perfectionism? Is it possible for a person with perfectionistic tendencies only to experience the positive outcomes without the negative or vice versa? The search for these answers motivates researchers to continue unpacking this complex construct.

One line of research that remains of interest particularly to those in the field of educational psychology is the relationship between aspects of perfectionism and academic outcomes. The research on perfectionism and academic outcomes, however, is more limited in scope than one might expect (Rice, Richardson, & Ray, 2016). The relatively limited research base may be attributed to the origins of perfectionism research in clinical and counseling psychology; researchers have overwhelmingly focused their investigations on the consequences of perfectionism on individuals' psychological adjustment and mental health. One might expect that there must have been a substantial increase in research on perfectionism and academic achievement in the last decade. Research literature searches, however, only yielded about 20 studies in the last decade that included perfectionism and a direct measure of academic achievement.

Additional attention to perfectionism and academic achievement is critical because of the amount of time that children and adolescents spend in schools in industrialized nations. School teachers have reported seeing early signs of perfectionism in children (Rice et al., 2016) and the heightened social comparisons to others in adolescence make it a key time period for the development of perfectionism (Flett, Hewitt, Oliver, & Macdonald, 2002). Perfectionistic traits may also be expressed to a greater degree in certain high-pressure environments. There is a growing concern that achievement pressures in high schools, colleges, and universities are contributing to poor psychological adjustment and underachievement (Leonard et al., 2015; Novotney, 2014). Perfectionism, as well as the need to appear perfect (i.e., perfectionistic self-presentation), has been identified as an important factor that may underlie students' problematic adjustment to academic demands (Flett & Hewitt, 2013).

Studies on perfectionism and academic outcomes will be described in detail throughout this book; however, the overall theme of the findings is a consistent general trend of perfectionistic strivings (i.e., having high personal standards for one's performance) relating to an increase in achievement and perfectionistic concerns (i.e., having concerns and fear surrounding one's performance) relating to a decrease in achievement. The purpose of this book is to extend this general understanding by unpacking the complexity of these relationships through an examination of factors that may exert additional influence. A historical overview of the perfectionism literature opens the book to discuss the different conceptualizations and measures of the construct over time. We then seek to provide an in-depth exploration of variables known to influence or be influenced by either perfectionism or achievement. These variables include driving forces such as parenting and attachment, personality, and motivation as well as outcome variables such as stress, burnout, anxiety, and procrastination. We discuss how these additional variables may influence the dynamics between perfectionism and achievement and highlight avenues for additional research to explore the intricacy of these relationships. An understanding of the complex interactive relationships of these variables with perfectionism and achievement is critical for guiding prevention and intervention efforts. In the final chapter, we propose a theoretical model for future work on perfectionism and academic achievement and discuss additional areas that, while less well researched, deserve attention for their potential influence on how perfectionism may impact academic achievement.

It is our hope that advanced students and their faculty mentors will see components of perfectionism that might be relevant to their discipline, and, as a result, devise ways to expand upon previous work on perfectionism and academic achievement. With additional empirical work on perfectionism and academic achievement, prevention and intervention efforts will hopefully more effectively target aspects of perfectionism that are problematic, allowing individuals to achieve in accordance with their potential.

CHAPTER 1

Perfectionism

History of Perfectionism Research

Throughout history, psychologists have recognized perfectionism as a complex phenomenon, a motivating force with a dark side casting a shadow on the seemingly positive strive toward excellence. Alfred Adler, one of the earliest psychologists to write about perfectionism, considered perfectionism to be an innate part of human nature, a central intensity without which life would be unimaginable (Adler, 1956). Adler contended that perfectionism may be healthy when directed toward maximizing one's potential or rooted in social concern for others. Other early theorists also shared this perspective, viewing the search for perfection as a positive influence fueling the development of one's potential or self-actualization (Dabrowski, 1964; Maslow, 1970; Spence & Helmreich, 1983).

Alder also acknowledged that perfectionism may be negative when accompanied by self-destructive tendencies. In keeping with this theory, Hamachek (1978) distinguished two forms of perfectionism: normal and neurotic. According to Hamachek, normal perfectionists are those who "derive a very real sense of pleasure from the labors of a painstaking effort and who feel free to be less precise as the situation permits" (p. 23). These normal perfectionists seek social approval, but this approval is not their fundamental reason for seeking perfection; rather, it serves as motivation for improving their performance. In contrast to normal perfectionists, Hamachek described neurotic perfectionists as those individuals who "demand a higher level of performance than [is] possible for them to obtain" (p. 28). Neurotic perfectionists never feel satisfied by their performance, and their motivation stems from a fear of failure rather than a need for achievement.

In 1980, Burns also attempted to clarify two different types of individuals, only one that he perceived as perfectionistic. He wrote:

> I want to make clear what I mean by perfectionism. I do not mean the healthy pursuit of excellence by men and women who take genuine pleasure in striving to meet high standards. Without concern for quality, life would seem shallow and true accomplishments would be rare. The perfectionists I am talking about are those whose standards are high beyond reach or reason, people who strain compulsively and unremittingly toward impossible goals and who measure their own worth entirely in terms of productivity and accomplishment. For these people the drive to excel can only be self-defeating. (Burns, 1980, p. 34)

Despite the different labels favored by Burns and Hamachek, they appear to be describing the same two groups of individuals. In his 1984 award address to the American Psychological Association, leading psychologist Asher Pacht echoed this duality. But similar to Burns, eschewed the label of "normal perfectionist" when describing individuals who carefully work to master their craft, stating, "The insidious nature of perfectionism leads me to use the label only when describing a kind of psychopathology" (Pacht, 1984, p. 387).

Measuring Perfectionism

Initial perceptions of perfectionism as related to psychopathology were based primarily on observations of people within clinical settings. Based on these clinical observations of the dual nature of perfectionism, clinical psychologists in academic institutions began to clarify the multifaceted nature of perfectionism and derive empirical methods to measure it during the 1990s. Two scales promoting multidimensional frameworks for studying perfectionism were simultaneously released from clinical psychologists (Frost, Marten, Lahart, & Rosenblate, 1990; Hewitt & Flett, 1991). Unfortunately, both scales bear the same name: Multidimensional Perfectionism Scale. Each scale attempted to capture the multidimensional nature of perfectionism but was focused on different dimensions of perfectionism.

Hewitt and Flett's (1991) Multidimensional Perfectionism Scale (herein referred to as HFMPS) takes into consideration both personal and social elements resulting in three different dimensions of perfectionism. While each dimension focuses on setting unrealistic standards and expectations, the dimensions vary in terms of who is setting the expectations and the object of those expectations. Hewitt and Flett defined those scoring high on the measure of self-oriented perfectionism as individuals who set unrealistic standards and expectations for themselves. They may not be concerned with others' (parents, teachers, peers, or bosses) expectations but rather have their own impractical high standards. In contrast, Hewitt and Flett defined those scoring high on the measure of socially prescribed perfectionism as individuals who perceive others as placing impossibly high standards or unrealistic expectations for their performance. Whether or not this view is accurate is irrelevant; the perception of pressure from others to reach unrealistic standards defines socially prescribed perfectionism. Finally, Hewitt and Flett defined those scoring high on the measure of other-oriented perfectionism as placing unrealistic expectations or standards for others' performance or behaviors.

In their seminal article establishing validity for their multidimensional measure, Hewitt and Flett (1991) recounted their studies across multiple populations (clinical and student) demonstrating differential relationships among the three dimensions of perfectionism with personality disorders and positive and negative indicators of psychological adjustment. Each perfectionism dimension—self-oriented, socially prescribed, and other-oriented—was related to a specific set of negative personality traits and symptoms of psychological maladjustment (Hewitt & Flett, 1991; Study 3). However, high standards for achievement were also positively associated with each perfectionism dimension. Perfectionism dimensions revealed different patterns: self-oriented perfectionism was correlated with self-importance for academic and performance standards, whereas socially prescribed perfectionism was correlated with academic and performance standards as being important to others. Results from the validity studies of the HFMPS captured the dual nature of perfectionism as positive and negative.

The other Multidimensional Perfectionism Scale, developed by Frost et al. (1990) (herein referred to as FMPS) tapped six different dimensions of the construct: personal standards, concern over mistakes, parental expectations, parental criticism, doubting actions, and organization.[1] The subscale, concern over mistakes, had the strongest link to negative affect (Frost, Heimberg, Holt, Mattia, & Neubauer, 1993), while the subscale of high personal standards and organization had the strongest relationships to adaptive work habits, motivation, and high achievement (Brown et al., 1999; Frost et al., 1990). Similar to the HFMPS, results that the subscales differentially correlated with either positive or negative outcomes offer support for the duality of perfectionism observed by Hamachek (1978), Burns (1980), and Pacht (1984).

Moving away from an emphasis on psychopathology, Slaney and Johnson (1992) attempted to focus on the positive aspects of perfectionism for the field of counseling psychology. Slaney and Johnson developed the Almost Perfect Scale (APS); however, the published scale still included an emphasis on the negative rather than the positive dimensions of perfectionism (Slaney, Rice, Mobley, Trippi, & Ashby, 2001). Consequently, Slaney and colleagues (2001) published a revised version of the APS. The following four criteria guided their revision of the original scale: (1) include only variables that defined perfectionism and exclude those variables that were seen as either causal, correlational, or illustrating the effects of perfectionism; (2) adhere closely to the empirical notions of positive and negative aspects of perfectionism; (3) closely relate to commonly held perceptions of perfectionism as indicated by dictionary definitions; and (4) be empirically sound. The results of their work yielded the Almost Perfect Scale-Revised (herein referred to as APS-R), a three-factor measure of perfectionism including high standards, discrepancy, and order. The high standards subscale measures the extreme nature of the personal standards that individuals with perfectionism set for themselves. The discrepancy subscale measures the negative aspect of perfectionism that centers on the perception that high personal standards are not being met. Finally, the order subscale measures orderliness as a defining feature of perfectionism. Whereas the order subscale was positively correlated with

---

[1] It should be noted that researchers have questioned the use of organization, parental expectations, and parental criticism as defining dimensions of perfectionism (Stoeber & Otto, 2006).

both self-esteem and worry, the high standards subscale was positively correlated with self-esteem and grade point average (GPA) and the discrepancy subscale was negatively correlated with self-esteem and GPA. The APS-R has offered a popular alternative for researchers in the field of perfectionism working with nonclinical populations.

Perfectionistic Strivings and Perfectionistic Concerns

Over the past 25 years, these three multidimensional perfectionism scales represent the most commonly used measures of trait perfectionism (Sirois & Molnar, 2016). Additional work on the APS-R, FMPS, and HFMPS since their publication has examined the factor structure of these measures both separately and in combination (Cox, Enns, & Clara, 2002; Frost et al., 1993; Rice, Lopez, & Vergara, 2005; Suddarth & Slaney, 2001). When item responses from undergraduates on the FMPS and HFMPS were analyzed, two factors were revealed: positive strivings (HFMPS self-oriented perfectionism, HFMPS other-oriented perfectionism, FMPS personal standards, and FMPS organization) and maladaptive evaluative concerns (HFMPS socially prescribed perfectionism, FMPS concern over mistakes, FMPS doubts about actions, FMPS parental expectations, and FMPS parental criticism) (Frost et al., 1993). With an undergraduate sample and a sample of adults from a clinical setting, Cox et al. (2002) reported good fit for a two-factor structure for maladaptive perfectionism (FMPS concern over mistakes, FMPS doubts about actions, FMPS parental criticism, HFMPS socially prescribed perfectionism) and adaptive perfectionism (FMPS personal standards, FMPS order, HFMPS self-oriented perfectionism) using their brief FMPS and HFMPS measures.

Two additional studies have also included the APS-R in factor analyses of the HFMPS and FMPS perfectionism measures (Rice et al., 2005; Suddarth & Slaney, 2001). Although additional factors were found in studies that included the APS-R (i.e., order and parental/social influences), both studies reported a maladaptive perfectionism factor (FMPS doubts about actions, FMPS concern over mistakes, and APS-R discrepancy) and an adaptive perfectionism factor (FMPS personal standards, HFMPS self-oriented perfectionism, and APS-R high standards)

(Rice et al., 2005; Suddarth & Slaney, 2001). Although adaptive and maladaptive perfectionism were used as labels to describe the two perfectionism dimensions, the terms were controversial largely due to the disputed notion that perfectionism is adaptive (Flett & Hewitt, 2006). In an effort to avoid controversial, value-laden terms such as adaptive and maladaptive, healthy and unhealthy, positive and negative, Stoeber and Otto (2006) used perfectionistic strivings and perfectionistic concerns to label the two dimensions in their literature review. In their review, the perfectionistic strivings term was used to summarize results across studies that examined specific subscales, and/or combination of the subscales, of self-oriented perfectionism from the HFMPS, personal standards and order from the FMPS, and high standards and order from the APS-R. The perfectionistic concerns term was used to summarize results across studies that examined specific subscales, and/or combination of the subscales, of socially prescribed perfectionism from the HFMPS, concern over mistakes and doubts about actions from the FMPS, and discrepancy from the APS-R. Parental expectations and parental criticism from the FMPS are associated with perfectionistic concerns, yet are not widely used as defining features of perfectionism (Stoeber & Otto, 2006). In the last 10 years, perfectionism researchers have largely adopted perfectionistic strivings and perfectionistic concerns as terms for the two dimensions of perfectionism.

In addition to articulating the commonly used terms of perfectionistic strivings and perfectionistic concerns, Stoeber and Otto (2006) also argued that perfectionistic strivings should be viewed as a positive form of perfectionism. In their review of studies that examined perfectionism, perfectionistic strivings were positively associated with positive affect, self-esteem, active coping, conscientiousness, extraversion, academic achievement, and decreased depression and anxiety, particularly when controlling for the statistical overlap with perfectionistic concerns. Stoeber and Otto concluded that, "…the perfectionistic strivings dimension is associated with positive characteristics and unrelated or even inversely related to those negative characteristics traditionally associated with perfectionism" (p. 312). Consistent with earlier theoretical orientations of neurotic perfectionism, perfectionistic concerns were associated with negative affect, neuroticism, obsessive-compulsive symptoms, depression, anxiety, and suicidal ideation (Stoeber & Otto, 2006). Empirical evidence and theoretical perspectives of perfectionistic strivings as a positive form of perfectionism and perfectionistic concerns as a negative form of perfectionism are predominant in the research literature, yet this dichotomy remains controversial (see recent edited books by Hewitt, Flett, & Mikail, 2017; Hill, 2016; Sirois & Molnar, 2016; Stoeber, 2017).

Shifting Conceptualization of Perfectionism

Perspectives of perfectionistic strivings as a positive form of perfectionism largely stems from empirical research that has employed data analytic techniques that separate perfectionistic strivings and perfectionistic concerns. Researchers who have objected to partialling perfectionistic concerns from perfectionistic strivings (i.e., statistically controlling for the overlapping variance of perfectionistic concerns when examining perfectionistic strivings) argue that core elements of perfectionism such as conditional self-acceptance and self-criticism are lost (Flett & Hewitt, 2014; Hill, 2014); however, others have defended the practice (Stoeber & Gaudreau, 2017). By statistically removing variance associated with the negative aspects of perfectionistic strivings, the perfectionistic strivings construct is more closely aligned with conscientiousness and striving for excellence, and thus, conceptually different from perfectionism (Hill, 2014).

In reality, a substantial number of people have high levels of both perfectionistic strivings and perfectionistic concerns. In an attempt to understand combinations of perfectionistic strivings and perfectionistic concerns, researchers have used data analytic methods to examine within-person variability of the two perfectionistic dimensions (i.e., group approach). Cluster analysis is a statistical technique that seeks to sort cases, or people, into groups that score similarly on a set of measures. Using cluster analysis, researchers have generally obtained three different groups of perfectionists: (1) a group with high perfectionistic strivings and low-to-medium perfectionistic concerns, (2) a group with high perfectionistic strivings and high perfectionistic concerns, and (3) a group with low perfectionistic strivings and low perfectionistic concerns (non-perfectionists). Using this tripartite model (Stoeber & Otto, 2006), groups of individuals with high perfectionistic strivings tend to have better psychological adjustment and achievement outcomes compared with groups of individuals with high perfectionistic strivings and high perfectionistic concerns (Gilman, Ashby, Sverko, Florell & Varjas, 2005; Grzegorek, Slaney, Franze, & Rice, 2004; Mobley, Slaney, & Rice, 2005; Rice, Ashby, & Gilman, 2011; Rice & Dellwo, 2002; Rice & Mirzadeh, 2000; Rice & Slaney, 2002).

In contrast to the tripartite model, Gaudreau and Thompson's (2010) 2 × 2 model of dispositional perfectionism examined four different subtypes of perfectionism: (1) high perfectionistic strivings and low perfectionistic concerns (pure perfectionistic strivings perfectionism), (2) low perfectionistic strivings and high perfectionistic concerns (pure perfectionistic concerns perfectionism), (3) high perfectionistic strivings and high perfectionistic concerns (mixed perfectionism), and (4) low perfectionistic strivings and low perfectionistic concerns (non-perfectionism). Gaudreau (2012) adopted a variable-centered data analysis approach based on regression to examine the four subtypes of perfectionism. Furthermore, four specific hypotheses are to be tested for positive outcomes for the 2 × 2 dispositional model of perfectionism: (1) pure perfectionistic strivings perfectionism will be greater than non-perfectionism; (2) non-perfectionism will be greater than pure perfectionistic concerns perfectionism; (3) mixed perfectionism will be greater than pure perfectionistic concerns perfectionism; and (4) pure perfectionistic strivings perfectionism will be greater than mixed perfectionism. Opposite relationships are hypothesized for negative outcomes. The model purports that pure perfectionistic strivings are more adaptive than non-perfectionism; pure perfectionistic concerns are the least adaptive outcome of the four types; and mixed perfectionism (i.e., high scores on both perfectionistic strivings and perfectionistic concerns) is more adaptive than pure perfectionistic concerns, but not as adaptive as pure perfectionistic strivings.

Recently, Stoeber (2014) endorsed the examination of both models in perfectionism research as a way to determine the potential interactive effects of perfectionistic strivings and perfectionistic concerns. With data that compares pure perfectionistic concerns to non-perfectionism, researchers can determine which model best supports the data. The tripartite model would be supported if the two groups show no differences (non-perfectionism and pure perfectionistic concerns do not differ on grades). If pure perfectionistic concerns have different associations with outcomes than non-perfectionism (e.g., non-perfectionism is associated with higher grades than pure perfectionistic concerns), the data supports the 2 × 2 model. Research on perfectionism and academic achievement thus far has supported the 2 × 2 model of dispositional perfectionism: pure perfectionistic concerns perfectionism, as measured by socially prescribed perfectionism, was associated with lower GPAs than non-perfectionism (Franche, Gaudreau, & Miranda, 2012). However, additional research is needed to examine these two different models in the area of perfectionism and academic achievement.

Perfectionism: Domain-general and Domain-specific

Our review of perfectionism theories has focused on the empirical research that has examined the three dominant measures of trait, or domain-general, perfectionism. Yet one continuing controversy is the extent to which perfectionism should be viewed as a general trait that is expressed equally across different life domains (e.g., academics, sports, work) or a disposition that is expressed only in specific domains (Hill, 2016; Stoeber & Stoeber, 2009). Offering a compromise to this dichotomy, Franche and Gaudreau (2016) have advocated for viewing perfectionism as a multilevel construct, with approaches to studying individual differences (i.e., between-persons) and individual variability (i.e., within-persons) providing complementary information for understanding perfectionism.

Although much of the research in the field has studied perfectionism as a domain-general trait, there is some empirical support that individuals have significantly different levels of perfectionism across different domains (Dunn, Causgrove Dunn, & McDonald, 2012; McArdle, 2010). To examine perfectionism across different domains, researchers have adapted the instructions and items for the trait perfectionism measures in order to ask participants to consider their perfectionistic traits only within a specific domain (Dunn et al., 2012; McArdle, 2010; Mitchelson & Burns, 1998). One study using this method found that intercollegiate athletes reported higher levels of perfectionism for sports on each subscale of the HFMPS compared to academics (Dunn, Gotwals, & Dunn, 2005). In another study, high ability students reported higher levels of perfectionism (i.e., total score on the FMPS minus organization) for academics compared to sports (McArdle, 2010). Finally, examining perfectionism across five different life domains (university/work, relationships, physical activity, home, and personal appearance) in university students, perfectionism related to achievement—university/work—was significantly higher than the other four domains (Haase, Prapavessis, & Owens, 2013).

Researchers have speculated that aspects of motivation and/or competence might underlie perfectionistic tendencies in certain domains (Flett, Hewitt, Oliver, & Macdonald, 2002). In the academic domain, McArdle (2010) reported that perfectionism in academics was correlated with perceived competence in academics and importance of academics in high-ability students; however, these relationships were not significant in additional regression analyses. In contrast, in the sample of intercollegiate athletes, Dunn et al. (2012) found that perceived competence in sports and importance of one's performance in sports predicted self-oriented perfectionism and socially prescribed perfectionism. Collectively, the results of these initial studies suggest the need for further research: to replicate the validity of domain-specific perfectionism across fields and to determine variables such as motivation and competency that may influence individual differences in domain-specific perfectionism.

Studies that have explored the possibility of domain-specific perfectionism suggest promising lines of future research, especially within the arena of academic achievement. However, some limitations must be addressed. For instance, even when examining perfectionism within a specific domain, researchers still average responses to survey items that inquire about general skills within a domain. Instead of displaying perfectionism across all academic work, students might be more likely to express perfectionism for assignments and evaluations in their major coursework compared to general courses and electives. Thus, future studies may use data analytic approaches to examine both between- and within-person variability (Franche & Gaudreau, 2016). Yet one lingering limitation of quantitative research in perfectionism is the paucity of information about the specific performance or achievement contexts used as a reference point by participants in completing self-report measures. Domain-specific measures of perfectionism in sports psychology such as the Sport Multidimensional

Perfectionism Scale-2 (Sport-MPS-2; Gotwals & Dunn, 2009) and the Multidimensional Inventory of Perfectionism in Sport (MIPS; Stoeber, Otto, & Stoll, 2006) narrow the specific performance contexts for research participants (Gotwals, 2016). However, in the academic domain, no specific perfectionism measures have been designed to target perfectionistic tendencies in academic work. Qualitative research may provide crucial information about the particular achievement situations that tend to enhance students' perfectionistic strivings and/or perfectionistic concerns. Additional research is needed to examine trait perfectionism and perfectionism across multiple academic situations and document the characteristics of those situations that may reveal students' perfectionistic tendencies.

Academic Achievement and Perfectionism

Surprisingly few studies have focused specifically on the two dimensions of perfectionism, perfectionistic strivings and perfectionistic concerns, and academic achievement outcomes. Following from the review published by Stoeber and Otto (2006), research from 2006 to 2016 on perfectionism and academic achievement was examined. Studies that have used the three major measures of perfectionism and a direct measure of academic achievement are presented in Table 1.1.

An analysis of the research studies highlighted in Table 1.1 indicates preliminary findings of interest. For example, perfectionistic strivings were consistently related to higher grades on exams (Bong, Hwang, Noh, & Kim, 2014; Stoeber, Haskew, & Scott, 2015), higher grades in specific courses or subjects (Shim, Rubenstein, & Drapeau, 2016; Stoeber & Rambow, 2007; Witcher, Alexander, Onwuebuzie, Collins, & Witcher, 2007), and higher GPAs (Blankstein, Dunkley, & Wilson, 2008; Damian, Stoeber, Negru-Subtirica, & Baban, 2016; Eum & Rice, 2011; Nounopoulos, Ashby, & Gilman, 2006; Shaunessy, Suldo, & Friedrich, 2011; Verner-Filion & Gaudreau, 2010). Additionally, significantly higher GPAs were also reported for students with perfectionistic strivings compared to non-perfectionists using a group approach such as cluster analysis or cut-off scores (Elion, Wang, Slaney, & French, 2012; Jaradat, 2013; Rice, Lopez, & Richardson, 2013; Rice, Ray, Davis, DeBlaere,

Table 1.1 Reviewed results on perfectionistic strivings and perfectionistic concerns for academic achievement

Study	Sample	Measure	Academic outcome	Results
		Dimensional Approach		
Nounopoulos, Ashby, & Gilman (2006)	166 adolescents (United States)	APS-R	GPA	PS was positively correlated with GPA; PC was negatively correlated with GPA
Stoeber & Rambow (2007)	121 adolescents (Germany)	MIPS (adapted for academic)	Grades in German, English, and math	PS was positively correlated with grades
Witcher, Alexander, Onwuebuzie, Collins, & Witcher (2007)	130 psychology graduate students (United States)	HFMPS	Midterm and final exams in graduate research methods course	PS was positively correlated with course grades; PC was negatively correlated with course grades
Blankstein, Dunkley, & Wilson (2008)	386 undergraduates (North America)	HFMPS FMPS APS-R	GPA	PS was positively correlated with GPA
Flett, Blankstein, & Hewitt (2009)	92 female undergraduates (Canada)	HFMPS	Class exam	PS had no relationship to exam performance; PC had a negative relationship with exam performance
Stornelli, Flett, & Hewitt (2009)	223 children and adolescents (Canada)	CAPS	Canadian Achievement Test	PS and PC had no relationship to reading and math test scores
Verner-Filion & Gaudreau (2010)	336 undergraduates	HFMPS short form (Cox, Enns, & Clara, 2002)	GPA	PS was positively correlated with GPA; PC was negatively correlated with GPA
Eum & Rice (2011)	134 undergraduates (United States)	APS-R	GPA	PS was positively correlated with GPA; PC was negatively correlated with GPA

Shaunessy, Suldo, & Friedrich (2011)	178 general education and 141 IB high school students (United States)	APS-R	GPA	PS was positively correlated with GPA in both groups; PC was negatively correlated with GPA in IB students only
Franche, Gaudreau, & Miranda (2012)	159 Asian Canadian and 538 European Canadian undergraduates	Short 10-item version of the HFMPS (Cox, Enns, & Clara, 2002)	GPA	Pure PS was associated with higher GPAs than NP; pure PC was associated with lower GPAs than NP; MP was associated with higher GPAs than pure PC; No difference between PS and MP
Gaudreau (2012)	98 undergraduates (Canada)	Short 10-item version of the HFMPS (Cox, Enns, & Clara, 2002)	GPA	Pure PS was associated with higher GPAs than NP; pure PC was associated with lower GPAs than NP; MP was associated with higher GPAs than pure PC; pure PS was associated with higher GPAs than MP
Bong, Hwang, Noh, & Kim (2014)	306 adolescents (Korea)	HFMPS	Final exam scores in math and English	PS had a positive relationship with exam grades; PC had no relationship with exam grades
Stoeber, Haskew, & Scott (2015)	100 undergraduates (United Kingdom)	HFMPS	Mock exam after 2–4 days on chapter from textbook	PS had a positive relationship to exam performance; PC had a negative relationship to exam performance
Shim, Rubenstein, & Drapeau (2016)	169 adolescents (United States)	FMPS	Math grade	PS was positively related to math grades; PC had no relationship with math grades
Damian, Stoeber, Negru-Subtirica, & Baban (2016)	487 adolescents (Romania)	CAPS	GPA	PS predicted increases in GPA; PC did not

(Continued)

Table 1.1 (Continued)

Study	Sample	Measure	Academic outcome	Results
			Group Approach	
Herman, Trotter, Reinke, & Ialongo (2011)	661 adolescents (United States)	CAPS	GPA	PCP had higher GPAs than PSP
Elion, Wang, Slaney, & French (2012)	219 African American undergraduates (United States)	APS-R	GPA	PSP had higher GPAs than NP; PCP did not differ on GPA from PSP or NP
Wang (2012)	348 undergraduates (Taiwan)	APS-R	Cumulative grades in college (100-point scale)	PSP had higher grades than PCP and NP; No differences between PCP and NP
Jaradat (2013)	419 high school students (Jordan)	APS-R	GPA	PSP had higher GPAs than PCP and NP; No differences between PCP and NP
Rice, Lopez, & Richardson (2013)	450 STEM majors (United States)	APS-R	GPA in STEM courses	PSP had higher STEM GPAs compared to NP; No differences in STEM GPAs between PCP and NP
Rice, Ray, Davis, DeBlaere, & Ashby (2015)	432 freshman STEM majors (United States)	APS-R FMPS	GPA in STEM courses	PSP under low stress had the highest STEM GPA; PCP under high stress had the lowest STEM GPA
Yang et al. (2016)	1,020 4th–12th grade students (China)	SAPS	Grade (3-point scale)	PSP had higher grade scores than PCP and NP

Note: Abbreviated terms include: (1) sample: [International Baccalaureate (IB); Science, Technology, Engineering, and Math (STEM)]; (2) measures: [Almost Perfect Scale-Revised (APS-R); Child and Adolescent Perfectionism Scale (CAPS); Hewitt and Flett Multidimensional Perfectionism Scale (HFMPS); Frost Multidimensional Perfectionism Scale (FMPS); Multidimensional Inventory of Perfectionism in Sport (MIPS); Short Almost Perfect Scale (SAPS)]; (3) outcomes: [GPA (self-report or documented)]; and (4) results: [perfectionistic strivings (PS); perfectionistic concerns (PC); mixed perfectionism (MP); perfectionistic strivings perfectionists (PSP); perfectionistic concerns perfectionists (PCP); non-perfectionists (NP)]

& Ashby, 2015; Wang, 2012; Yang et al., 2016). However, the group approach also revealed that students with perfectionistic concerns did not differ significantly on GPAs than non-perfectionists (Elion et al., 2012; Jaradat, 2013; Rice et al., 2013; Wang, 2012; Yang et al., 2016). Only one study of sixth grade, urban African American adolescents found the opposite trend: students with perfectionistic concerns had higher GPAs than students with perfectionistic strivings (Herman, Trotter, Reinke, & Ialongo, 2011). In contrast, using the dimensional approach, numerous studies reported the negative relationship between perfectionistic concerns and academic achievement (Eum & Rice, 2011; Flett, Blankstein, & Hewitt, 2009; Stoeber et al., 2015; Nounopoulos et al., 2006; Shaunessy et al., 2011; Verner-Filion & Gaudreau, 2010; Witcher et al., 2007). Examining the 2 × 2 model of dispositional perfectionism and academic achievement, pure perfectionistic strivings perfectionism (high self-oriented and low socially prescribed) was associated with higher GPAs than non-perfectionism, whereas pure perfectionistic concerns perfectionism (high socially prescribed and low self-oriented) was associated with lower GPAs than non-perfectionism. Pure perfectionistic concerns perfectionism was also associated with lower GPAs than mixed perfectionism (high self-oriented and high socially prescribed) (Franche, Gaudreau, & Miranda, 2012; Gaudreau, 2012). Although three of the four hypotheses were supported for the 2 × 2 model of dispositional perfectionism, Franche et al. (2012) found no difference between GPAs for pure perfectionistic strivings perfectionism and mixed perfectionism whereas Gaudreau (2012) did.

In summary, perfectionistic strivings support academic achievement, particularly when controlling for the overlapping variance with perfectionistic concerns. In contrast, perfectionistic concerns negatively related to achievement (Eum & Rice, 2011; Flett et al., 2009; Stoeber et al., 2015; Nounopoulos et al., 2006; Shaunessy et al., 2011; Verner-Filion & Gaudreau, 2010; Witcher et al., 2007). Consistent with findings using the dimensional approach, individuals with perfectionistic concerns also had lower GPAs than individuals with perfectionistic strivings; however, they did not differ from non-perfectionists on GPA when the group approach was used (Elion et al., 2012; Jaradat, 2013; Rice et al., 2013; Wang, 2012).

Summary

Changes in the conceptualization and measurement of perfectionism over time present challenges in interpreting research findings. This challenge serves as a reminder of the importance of considering research findings within context: a central theme throughout this book. The academic context represents a fundamental and overarching life domain for children, adolescents, and young adults. Moreover, national and community initiatives to promote life-long learning and professional development requirements in many careers also indicate that the process of learning and education continues throughout the lifespan. In any educational setting at any age, students with perfectionistic tendencies will approach academic evaluations and challenges in ways that are different from others. Understanding additional factors that may mediate (i.e., account for the relationship between perfectionism and academic achievement) or moderate (i.e., affects the direction and/or strength of the relationship between perfectionism and academic achievement) are important avenues for future research and will be critical in devising approaches to help perfectionists maximize their achievement.

CHAPTER 2

Attachment, Personality, and Perfectionism

Researchers interested in understanding the origins of perfectionism have examined personality and attachment as two contributing factors (Hewitt, Flett, & Mikail, 2017). Incorporating elements of personality and attachment, Blatt proposed a model of personality development that included self-definition and relatedness as primary dimensions (Blatt, 2004; Blatt & Levy, 2003; Blatt & Luyten, 2009; Blatt & Zuroff, 1992). Self-definition refers to cognitions, emotions, and actions toward the self, whereas relatedness refers to cognitions, emotions, and actions toward others. Yet personality development depends on the dynamic interaction of self-definition and relatedness across the lifespan: a mature and integrated sense of self develops within the context of personal relationships and personal relationships become more intimate and satisfying with the development of a mature sense of self and identity (Blatt & Levy, 2003; Kopala-Sibley, Zuroff, Hermanto, & Joyal-Desmarais, 2016). According to Blatt (1974), self-definition and relatedness factors influence personality development and may confer vulnerabilities to psychopathology (see Kopala-Sibley & Zuroff, 2014 for a review).

Recognizing the theoretical significance of self-definition and relatedness for perfectionism, Flett, Hewitt, Oliver, and Macdonald (2002) integrated self-definition (temperament, personality) factors and relatedness (attachment status, family) factors into a theoretical model on the development of perfectionism. The self-definition and relatedness model of personality development provides an organizational framework for this chapter: in the first section, research on perfectionism and attachment status (relatedness) will be reviewed, and in the second section, research on personality (self-definition) will be reviewed.

Attachment Theory and Perfectionism

According to Blatt (1974), personality traits that might make individuals vulnerable to poor mental health may be traced back to primary caregivers who are emotionally unavailable, overprotective, or may use the child for their own emotional needs. Any of these types of relatedness to primary caregivers may lead to children's failure to develop stable, internal representations for relationships, leading to excessive dependency on others and need for approval and recognition. Blatt's (1974) relatedness construct in his theory of personality development borrowed heavily from attachment theory (Bowlby, 1980, 1988). Broadly speaking, attachment has been defined as close affectionate ties that provide an individual with a sense of security (Ainsworth, 1989; Bowlby, 1988). Bowlby (1980) contended that secure and insecure forms of attachment are manifestations of how individuals represent information about their relationships with primary caregivers (i.e., responsiveness, warmth). Schematic representation of this knowledge is referred to as an internal working model and is refined and elaborated as infants interact with their caregivers. Internal working models serve as a guide for interpreting events and forming expectations about relationships. Infants with sensitive, responsive caregivers will likely conclude that people are dependable; therefore, developing a working model that other people can be trusted. Infants with insensitive, neglectful, or abusive caregivers will likely conclude that people are not trustworthy; therefore, developing a working model that other people are unresponsive to their needs. Infants also develop a working model of the self as a result of their caregiving experiences. Infants whose caregivers are responsive to their needs will likely conclude that they are worthy and lovable but infants whose signals are ignored by their caregivers may conclude that they are unworthy of love.

Attachment theory proposes that experience with caregivers early in life establishes the formation for internal working models leading to secure or insecure attachment. Yet research on attachment and perfectionism has been mainly conducted with undergraduates. When conducting research on attachment with adults, researchers must rely on retrospective reports based on memories about participants' relationships with their primary caregiver. Such methods are not ideal to fully understand the attachment–perfectionism connection, but results from studies with adults will inform future research on attachment and perfectionism in children and adolescents.

Research has supported a relationship between insecure attachment and perfectionism, despite discrepancies in the ways both attachment and perfectionism were measured. For example, Andersson and Perris (2000) found a relationship between insecure attachment and perfectionism, as measured by the Dysfunctional Attitudes Scale, which taps self-critical perfectionism (Hautzinger, Luka, & Trautman, 1986). Similarly, Rice and Lopez (2004) found insecure adult attachment, as measured by the Adult Attachment Questionnaire (Simpson, Rholes, & Nelligan, 1992), predicted perfectionistic concerns, as measured by combining concern over mistakes and doubts about actions from the FMPS (Frost Multidimensional Perfectionism Scale; Frost, Marten, Lahart, & Rosenblate, 1990). Speirs Neumeister and Finch (2006) also found that insecure attachment, as measured by the Relationship Questionnaire (Crowell, Fraley, & Shaver, 1999), was associated with higher levels of self-oriented and socially prescribed perfectionism from the HFMPS (Hewitt and Flett Multidimensional Perfectionism Scale; Hewitt & Flett, 1991). Finally, using the discrepancy subscale of the APS-R (Almost Perfect Scale-Revised; Slaney, Rice, Mobley, Trippi, & Ashby, 2001), two additional studies also found a positive relationship between insecure attachment and perfectionistic concerns (Ulu & Tezer, 2010; Wei, Heppner, Russell, & Young, 2006). Thus, researchers have consistently reported a connection between insecure attachment and perfectionistic concerns.

Bartholomew and Horowitz (1991) took Bowlby's (1980) concept of secure and insecure attachment and applied it to the study of adult attachment styles. By crossing the two dimensions of working models of self and others with positive and negative experiences, researchers developed four styles of attachment: one secure form and three insecure forms: preoccupied, fearful, and dismissing. Secure individuals are characterized as believing they are lovable and believing others are generally accepting and responsive. Preoccupied individuals maintain a sense of unworthiness but evaluate others positively, resulting in striving for self-acceptance by gaining the approval of others. Fearful individuals do not believe they are worthy of being loved, viewing others as untrustworthy and rejecting.

Finally, dismissing individuals have a sense of worthiness, but they distrust others, causing them to protect themselves against disappointment by avoiding close relationships.

Insecure attachment and perfectionistic concerns share an emphasis on seeking approval from others and being hypervigilant to the possibility of rejection (Chen, Hewitt, & Flett, 2015). For example, the descriptions of individuals who are classified as having a preoccupied attachment style (Bartholomew & Horowitz, 1991) and those who are classified as socially prescribed perfectionists (Hewitt & Flett, 1991) are conceptually similar. In both cases, individuals are motivated to achieve others' acceptance, fear the disapproval of others, and experience a high degree of self-blame when they fail to gain the acceptance of others. Additionally, Hewitt and Flett (1991) also described self-oriented perfectionists as harboring self-blame for their mistakes that may also be indicative of an insecure attachment based on a negative model of self. Low self-worth and conditional self-worth based on achievement performance are hallmarks of preoccupied insecure attachment and perfectionistic concerns (Bartholomew & Horowitz, 1991; Burns, 1980; Flett & Hewitt, 2002; Frost et al., 1995).

Another model of attachment has also been studied through an examination of component factors associated with insecure attachment. Brennan, Clark, and Shaver (1998) analyzed 60 attachment subscales using factor analysis and found two factors of anxiety and avoidance. The avoidance factor centers on the extent to which individuals prefer to be psychologically and emotionally independent and as a result limit their intimacy with others. The anxiety factor centers on the extent to which individuals worry about their access to other people including whether or not other individuals might abandon them. Incorporating dimensions conceptually similar to avoidance and anxiety, the Adult Attachment Scale (Collins & Read, 1990) measures attachment into three dimensions: closeness, dependency, and anxiety. Similar to the avoidance factor of Brennen et al., the closeness dimension refers to the extent to which individuals are comfortable with closeness and intimacy and the dependency dimension focuses on the extent to which individuals are comfortable depending on others and believing others will be available when needed. The anxiety dimension focuses on the extent to which individuals are worried others will reject or abandon them.

The first two dimensions (closeness and dependency) correlate strongly with one another, and their description is theoretically consistent with the avoidance factor of attachment (Brennan et al., 1998). Likewise, the description of the third factor, anxiety, is theoretically consistent with the anxiety factor (Brennan et al., 1998).

Fear of closeness, fear of dependency, and fear of loss were examined in relation to perfectionism across aggregated daily reports of attachment as well as instability indices of attachment (Dunkley, Berg, & Zuroff, 2012). Whereas previous research has mainly explored attachment from a trait perspective (i.e., treating it as a fixed variable), Dunkley et al. (2012) explored attachment from the perspective of a state capable of changing daily depending on the influence of other contextual variables. Dunkley et al. also used three measures of perfectionism—DEQ (Depressive Experiences Questionnaire; Blatt, D'Afflitti, & Quinlan, 1976), HFMPS, and FMPS—to obtain perfectionistic strivings and perfectionistic concerns. After controlling for perfectionistic strivings, perfectionistic concerns strongly related to the three dimensions of attachment: fear of closeness, fear of dependency, and fear of loss (Collins & Read, 1990) for both trait and state measurements of attachment (Dunkley et al., 2012).

Of all the studies reviewed, only one found a relationship between secure attachment and perfectionistic strivings. In this study, Rice and Mirzadeh (2000) used cluster analysis to classify individuals as perfectionistic strivings perfectionists, perfectionistic concerns perfectionists, or non-perfectionists using the FMPS. The Relationship Questionnaire (Crowell et al., 1999) was used to measure secure attachment to mothers and fathers. Using logistic regression, they could correctly classify 96 percent of perfectionistic strivings perfectionists when their mother attachment scores were known compared to only 31 percent of the perfectionistic concerns perfectionists in Study 1, with 78 percent and 62 percent, respectively, in a replication analysis in Study 2. The average score for mother attachment was much higher for the perfectionistic strivings perfectionists than the perfectionistic concerns perfectionists in both studies (Rice & Mirzadeh, 2000). Thus, individuals with secure attachments to their mothers were more likely to be perfectionistic strivings perfectionists than perfectionistic concerns perfectionists. However, it should be noted that this study was different than other studies in its use of person-centered data analysis and the measures of attachment and perfectionism.

The relationship between secure attachment and perfectionism is not well understood. Secure individuals may be less likely to adopt perfectionistic concerns because they have a positive view of themselves and others and do not make their self-worth contingent on their achievements. But what would lead individuals with secure attachments to develop exceedingly high perfectionistic strivings? Rice, Lopez, and Vergara (2005) suggested that high parental expectations combined with warmth instead of criticism might predict both secure attachment and perfectionistic strivings. As support for this hypothesis, secure attachment to mothers was related to membership in the perfectionistic strivings cluster (Rice & Mirzadeh, 2000). In another study, perfectionistic strivings were negatively correlated with attachment anxiety and attachment avoidance (Gnilka, Ashby, & Noble, 2013). Other studies, however, have not found this relationship. After controlling for perfectionistic concerns, no relationship between perfectionistic strivings and fear of closeness, fear of dependency, and fear of loss was found (Dunkley et al., 2012). Similarly, Ulu and Tezer (2010) found no correlation between high standards and either anxiety or avoidance attachment. Much more research is needed before a definitive conclusion on the relationship between secure attachment and perfectionism can be reached.

Several studies have examined the complex mediator and moderator relationships among attachment, perfectionism, and various measures of psychological well-being including depression, helplessness, and life satisfaction. The discrepancy subscale, a measure of perfectionistic concerns from the APS-R, fully mediated the relationship between adult attachment avoidance and depression and partially mediated the relationship between adult attachment anxiety and depression (Wei, Mallinckrodt, Russell, & Abraham, 2004). Likewise, Gnilka et al. (2013) also found discrepancy mediated the relationship between adult attachment and depression, hopelessness, and life satisfaction. Ineffective coping might help explain these results: discrepancy and ineffective coping mediated the relationship between attachment and depression (Wei et al., 2006). On the other hand, high standards were negatively correlated with attachment anxiety and attachment avoidance and mediated the relationship between avoidant adult attachment and hopelessness and life satisfaction (Gnilka et al., 2013). Perfectionistic strivings may reduce the likelihood of individuals withdrawing from intimate relationships and may mitigate feelings of hopelessness and increase life satisfaction.

The Social Disconnection Model

Building on earlier work on attachment and personality disorders, Hewitt, Flett, Sherry, and Caelian (2006) developed and elaborated on the Social Disconnection model. Within the Social Disconnection model, perfectionistic concerns and perfectionistic self-presentation develop as a result of problematic relationships with primary attachment figures. This condition leads to insecure attachment with others, a sense of shame, and unfulfilled needs for acceptance and approval. In this model, perfectionistic self-presentation refers to the desire for individuals to appear perfect in the eyes of others (Hewitt et al., 2003). Perfectionistic self-presentation has three facets: perfectionistic self-promotion, which refers to public promotion of one's supposedly perfect image; non-display of imperfection, which refers to the avoidance of behavioral displays of one's perceived imperfection; and nondisclosure of imperfection, which refers to the avoidance of verbal disclosures of imperfection.

Two studies examined the relationship between perfectionistic self-presentation and attachment that supported the Social Disconnection model. Chen and colleagues (Chen et al., 2012) examined the relationship between attachment, perfectionistic self-presentation, and social disconnect among adolescents. Each of the three facets of perfectionistic self-presentation correlated with social disconnection, and fearful attachment was related to the non-disclosure facet of perfectionistic self-presentation. Non-disclosure of imperfections partially mediated the relationship between fearful attachment and social disconnect. Socially prescribed perfectionism and perfectionistic self-presentation were positively related to the need to belong, shame, and insecure attachment styles (Chen, Hewitt, & Flett, 2015). Additionally, relationships between preoccupied attachment and interpersonal components of perfectionism (socially prescribed and self-presentation perfectionism) were mediated by a strong need for belongingness and shame. Hence, insecure attachment may contribute to perfectionists' need for acceptance and interpersonal connections (Chen et al., 2012). The significant associations between attachment and perfectionistic self-presentation support the notion that perfectionistic behaviors have developmental origins in early life (Chen et al., 2012; Hewitt et al., 2017) and highlight the need to examine the quality of attachment in relationships for individuals with perfectionistic concerns (Chen et al., 2015).

Future Research on Attachment and Perfectionism in the Academic Context

Attachment status and perfectionism research has solely focused on psychological outcomes. No research could be found that has tried to examine relationships among attachment status, perfectionism, and academic achievement. As such, this is an area ripe for future research. Research on attachment and perfectionism has been mainly conducted with undergraduates, meaning that researchers must rely on retrospective reports based on memories about participants' relationships with their primary caregiver. Thus, the effects of attachment status on perfectionism have likely been underestimated in previous research (Hewitt et al., 2017). Longitudinal research that establishes attachment style to primary caregivers and follows children through their tenure as students is needed to investigate emergent perfectionism and its influence on academic outcomes.

Within such longitudinal studies, researchers should also consider examining the expectations and criticism that students experience from important people outside of the family. Beyond primary caregivers, students may also form close relationships with teachers, coaches, and mentors who may also influence the development and/or enhanced expression of perfectionistic traits (Appleton & Curran, 2016; Flett et al., 2002; Perera & Chang, 2015; Shih, 2013). Future studies of perfectionism need to also inquire about the perfectionistic expectations and nature of criticism from other important people in the lives of children and adolescents.

Personality and Perfectionism

Whereas attachment and relatedness represent one dimension of personality development, according to Blatt's model, self-definition represents another component. Self-definition would include the adoption of both broad, higher level personality traits as well as narrow, lower level personality traits such as perfectionism (Hill, 2016). Self-definition has been found to be a higher-order factor composed of self-criticism and autonomy in factor analytic studies (Dunkley, Blankstein, Zuroff, Lecce, & Hui, 2006; Dunkley, Zuroff, & Blankstein, 2006). When individuals are delayed in developing a stable self-definition, likely due to excessive dependency on others, then they are likely to develop high levels of self-criticism (Kopala-Sibley et al., 2016), a major characteristic of perfectionism (Dunkley, Berg, & Zuroff, 2012). One widely examined area of research has been the extent to which perfectionism is related to self-definition involving broad, higher level personality traits (see Stoeber, Corr, Smith, & Saklofske, 2017, for a review). The majority of research on broad personality traits and perfectionism has focused on two major personality theories: Reinforcement sensitivity theory (RST) and the Big Five theory of personality.

Reinforcement Sensitivity Theory (RST) of Personality and Perfectionism

Gray's RST of personality proposes that the sensitivity of neurobiological systems that respond to reward and punishment underlie individual differences in personality traits such as anxiety (Gray, 1991). Integrating Gray's theory based on animal research, Carver and White (1994) developed a scale to measure two of the original three subsystems proposed by Gray (1991): (1) Behavioral Inhibition System (BIS) thought to be sensitive to punishment, non-rewards, and novelty and inhibit behavior toward goals that might result in unpleasant outcomes and (2) Behavioral Activation System (BAS) thought to be sensitive to reward, non-punishment and escape from punishment and propel behavior toward goals that might result in pleasurable outcomes. Factor analysis revealed that the BAS construct could be further divided into three subscales: BAS-drive (i.e., persistence toward goals), BAS-fun seeking (i.e., relative impulsivity in pursuit of goals), and BAS-reward responsiveness (i.e., strength of positive response to obtaining or anticipation of goals) (Carver & White, 1994). To date, studies that have examined the BIS/BAS and perfectionism have used the Carver and White (1994) conceptualization and measure of BIS/ BAS (Chang et al., 2007; O'Connor & Forgan, 2007; Randles, Flett, Nash, MacGregor, & Hewitt, 2010; Rasmussen, Elloit, & O'Connor, 2012; Turner & Turner, 2011), with the exception of one study (Stoeber & Corr, 2015).

Perhaps due to the use of the same measure for BIS/BAS, researchers have reported fairly consistent relationships between BIS/BAS and perfectionism. Sensitivity to punishment (BIS) significantly predicted perfectionistic strivings and perfectionistic concerns, even when different perfectionism measures were used (Chang et al., 2007; O'Connor & Forgan, 2007; Randles et al., 2010; Rasmussen et al., 2012; Stoeber & Corr, 2015; Turner & Turner, 2011). Using the FMPS, personal standards and doubts about actions were related to BIS, but not concern over mistakes (Chang et al., 2007). The BIS was also related to self-oriented and socially prescribed perfectionism across numerous studies (O'Connor & Forgan, 2007; Randles et al., 2010; Rasmussen et al., 2012; Turner & Turner, 2011). Being hypersensitive to potential negative consequences and avoiding situations that might result in negative outcomes seems to overlap conceptually with the perfectionistic concerns. Yet perfectionistic strivings also related to a heightened sensitivity to negative outcomes and cautious behavioral tendencies in response to potential negative outcomes. Individuals with perfectionism seem to have an underlying personality dimension to avoid situations that might result in negative consequences such as criticism, failure, and embarrassment.

In contrast to the relationship with the BIS, perfectionistic strivings and perfectionistic concerns had different relationships with the three BAS subscales (Carver & White, 1994). Self-oriented perfectionism was positively related to BAS-drive (O'Connor & Forgan, 2007; Randles et al., 2010). BAS-drive was also positively related to concern over mistakes and doubts about actions from the FMPS (Chang et al., 2007). Socially prescribed perfectionism had a negative relationship with BAS-fun seeking

(O'Connor & Forgan, 2007) and a positive relationship to BAS-reward responsiveness (Randles et al., 2010).

Although the results of the BIS, BAS, and perfectionism seem contradictory, they support the approach-avoidance conflict associated with perfectionism (Fletcher & Speirs Neumeister, 2012; Flett & Hewitt, 2006). In other words, individuals with perfectionism are driven toward positive aspects of achievement, yet live in fear of the potential negative consequences of failing to achieve such as criticism, guilt, and shame from themselves and/or others. In fact, anxiety disorders in humans have recently been studied using an approach-avoidance conflict paradigm (Aupperle & Paulus, 2010; Bach et al., 2014). Given approach-avoidance tendencies and the anxiety provoked by them, claims for perfectionistic strivings as a positive form of perfectionism seem less convincing. Individuals with both types of perfectionism have approach-avoidance behavioral profiles in response to challenging and novel situations when there are no guarantees of positive consequences and potential for negative consequences.

Perfectionistic strivings and perfectionistic concerns also had significant relationships with both BIS and BAS dimensions using the RST-Personality Questionnaire (Corr & Cooper, 2016) based on Gray and McNaughton's (2000) revised RST. According to revised RST (Gray & McNaughton, 2000), three neurological systems underlie behavioral approach and avoidance tendencies: BIS, BAS, and Flight-Fright-Freeze system (FFFS). Although the BAS was not revised, the BIS from the original theory was differentiated into the FFFS and BIS. The two inhibition systems are activated to varying degrees depending on whether aversive stimuli can be avoided or cannot be avoided. For stimuli that can be avoided, the FFFS is activated in response to aversive stimuli, whereas the BIS is activated in response to aversive stimuli that must be approached. Consider the case of an extremely demanding professor for a required course. Students with high BIS activation would likely engage in procrastination and experience anxiety surrounding assignments and exams for this course, yet remain enrolled in the course. In contrast, students with high FFFS activation would likely drop the course and try to find another professor.

Based on the revised RST and including the FFFS, the RST-Personality Questionnaire (Corr & Cooper, 2016) consists of six subscales: FFFS,

BIS, BAS-reward interest (i.e., seeking positive outcomes), BAS-drive persistence, BAS-reward reactivity (i.e., thrill attached to positive outcomes), and BAS-impulsivity. Using the HFMPS and controlling for each type of perfectionism, self-oriented and socially prescribed perfectionism were correlated with BIS, consistent with previous research (Stoeber & Corr, 2015). Self-oriented perfectionism was also correlated with FFFS and BAS-reward interest, BAS-reward reactivity, and BAS-drive persistence. In contrast, socially prescribed perfectionism was negatively correlated with BAS-drive persistence and positively correlated with BAS-impulsivity (Stoeber & Corr, 2015). Although replication is needed, the RST-Personality Questionnaire (Corr & Cooper, 2016) may offer a method to examine more specific elements of approach-avoidance tendencies in the personalities of students with perfectionism.

In particular, the BAS-impulsivity and perfectionistic concerns relationship has important implications for students with deficits in executive functioning skills (i.e., impulse control, attention, working memory) in the academic context. To our knowledge, there has been only one study of temperament, executive functioning and perfectionism in children. Affrunti, Gramszlo, and Woodruff-Borden (2016) examined 7- to 13-year-old children on measures of perfectionism completed by children (Children and Adolescent Perfectionism Scale; Flett et al., 1997) and the fear subscale of the Temperament in Middle Childhood Questionnaire (Simonds & Rothbart, 2004) and the Behavioral Rating Inventory of Executive Functions (BRIEF; Gioia, Isquith, Guy, & Kenworthy, 2000) completed by parents. Only the interaction of children's fearful temperament, which overlaps conceptually with BIS and FFFS in adults, and cognitive shift (i.e., the ability to flexibly solve problems and alternate attention) predicted perfectionistic concerns (Affrunti et al., 2016). Children with fearful temperaments and lower ability to shift their attention had higher levels of perfectionistic concerns. According to Affrunti et al. (2016), deficits in shifting attention might lead to perseveration on mistakes and failures and/or not meeting the standards of others. Students who are hyperfocused on failures in combination with avoidance behavioral tendencies will likely steer clear of novel and challenging academic tasks, even though they might have the intellectual ability to be successful.

Individuals with high sensitivity to negative outcomes such as criticism, mistakes, and failure are likely to develop perfectionism, leading them to avoid novel and/or challenging tasks. Whereas individuals with perfectionistic strivings might be able to offset avoidance tendencies, or at least to counterbalance them with approach tendencies, avoidance tendencies may be the dominant behavioral style for individuals with perfectionistic concerns. Perfectionistic concerns contributed unique variance to the prediction of negative outcomes such as worry, rumination, and suicidal thinking beyond the effects of BIS (Chang et al., 2007; Randles et al., 2010). Controlling for BIS, concern about mistakes and doubts about actions were still significant predictors of worry (Chang et al., 2007) and socially prescribed perfectionism still significantly contributed to the prediction of rumination (Randles et al., 2010). Socially prescribed perfectionism also fully mediated the relationship between BIS and suicidal thinking in a sample of college students (O'Connor & Forgan, 2007) and a sample of patients admitted to the hospital following a suicide attempt (Rasmussen et al., 2012). Although individuals with perfectionistic strivings are highly sensitive to negative outcomes, they nevertheless also demonstrate a strong drive to seek potential rewards and positive outcomes. This strong approach drive may buffer against the worry, rumination, and suicidal thinking associated with perfectionistic concerns.

Future Research on RST and Perfectionism in the Academic Context

Worry and rumination associated with perfectionistic concerns, beyond the BIS, will also likely contribute to reduced academic focus and achievement. However, much more work is needed to explain connections among BIS/BAS, perfectionism, and academic achievement. Studies that examined all three constructs could not be located, although two studies were found that suggest directions for future research. BIS/BAS tendencies are related to academic study: the BIS was associated with overcommitment to studies and exhaustion, whereas the BAS was associated with study engagement, less exhaustion, and positively with grades (van Beek, Kranenburg, Taris, & Schaufeli, 2013). Although no measure of perfectionism was used, Liew, Lench, Kao, Yeh, and Kwok (2014) asked undergraduates to rate evaluative threat after a math test—the degree that they felt threatened by the test and that they feared failing the test— as well as measures of BIS and reported math grades in college courses and college entrance exams. Evaluative threat appears to overlap with per- fectionistic concerns. After accounting for gender differences, evaluative threat mediated the relationship between avoidance tendencies and low math achievement in college courses and college entrance exams (Liew et al., 2014). Students with avoidance personalities, like students with perfectionistic concerns, will focus on potential negative consequences of evaluations and experienced enhanced threat for evaluations, likely reduc- ing their ability to focus on academic tasks and studying. Regarding the general trend of perfectionistic strivings related to increased academic achievement and perfectionistic concerns related to decreased academic achievement, factors associated with approach-avoidance tendencies might help to explain this trend. However, much more research is needed before fully understanding the dynamics of how broad personality traits, in combination with perfectionism, impact specific academic outcomes.

Big Five Model of Personality and Perfectionism

In contrast to the biologically based RST, the Five-Factor model of per- sonality is based on psychometric analyses of how individuals describe their cognitive, affective, and behavioral tendencies using specific traits or facets (Costa & McCrae, 1992, 1995; McCrae & Costa, 1987). The development of the Big Five theory of personality and its measurement has a long history in psychology (see John, Naumann, & Soto, 2008 for a review). But in short, five domains (extroversion, agreeableness, con- scientiousness, neuroticism, and openness/intellect) were revealed using factor analysis of self-report and/or peer report of ratings on various spe- cific facets (Costa & McCrae, 1992). Extroversion describes individuals who are excitable, talkative, social, and highly emotionally expressive. Agreeableness describes individuals who are trusting, exhibit prosocial behaviors, and are kind and compassionate toward others. Conscien- tiousness describes individuals who devote high levels of attention to details in their work, have high levels of effortful control, and display goal directed behaviors. Neuroticism describes individuals who frequently display negative affect, unstable moods, and are lower in emotional control. Openness describes individuals who are high in curiosity, creativity, and open-mindedness.

There has been a wealth of research on the Big Five personality traits and perfectionism (Basirion, Majid & Jelas, 2014; Cruce, Pashak, Handel, Munz, & Gfeller, 2012; DeCuyper, Claes, Hermans, Pieters, & Smits, 2015; Egan, Vinciguerra, & Mazzucchelli, 2015; Rice, Ashby, & Slaney, 2007; Stoeber, Otto, & Dalbert, 2009; Ulu & Tezer, 2010). Because of the consistent findings across samples and methods, it is widely accepted that perfectionistic concerns are related to neuroticism and perfectionistic strivings are related to conscientiousness (see Stoeber, Corr, Smith, & Saklofske, 2017, for a review). Although the perfectionistic strivings-conscientiousness and perfectionistic concerns-neuroticism connections have been repeatedly documented, relationships between perfectionistic dimensions and agreeableness, extraversion, and openness are less straightforward and vary across different samples and methods. Moreover, the age group of the samples studied also seems to impact research findings; thus, we will review studies with adolescents, undergraduates, and adults separately.

In one of the few longitudinal studies, Stoeber et al. (2009) examined perfectionism and personality traits at two time points in 14- to 19-year-old German adolescents. Self-oriented perfectionism was correlated with conscientiousness and socially prescribed perfectionism was positively correlated with neuroticism and negatively correlated with extraversion, openness, and agreeableness. Moreover, conscientiousness at Time 1 predicted self-oriented perfectionism at Time 2 (Stoeber et al., 2009). Perfectionistic strivings also predicted conscientiousness and openness and perfectionistic concerns predicted neuroticism in 16-year-old Malaysian gifted students (Basirion et al., 2014), using each of the subscales from the FMPS for perfectionistic strivings (personal standards and organization) and perfectionistic concerns (concern over mistakes, doubts about actions, parental expectations, parental criticism).

When examining research on perfectionism and the Big Five personality traits in undergraduates, there is additional evidence for the perfectionistic strivings-conscientiousness and perfectionistic concerns-neuroticism connections (Cruce et al., 2012; DeCuyper et al., 2015; Egan et al., 2015; Rice et al., 2007; Ulu & Tezer, 2010). Using the three different measures of perfectionism (APS-R, FMPS, and HFMPS), each measure of perfectionistic strivings was significantly correlated with conscientiousness and each measure of perfectionistic concerns was significantly correlated with neuroticism (Rice et al., 2007). Regression analyses revealed that, even after controlling for the other Big Five personality constructs, the discrepancy subscale from the APS-R still predicted neuroticism and high standards subscale from the APS-R still predicted conscientiousness (Rice et al., 2007). Cruce et al. (2012) also reported that conscientious perfectionism, a measure of perfectionistic strivings from the Perfectionism Inventory Scale (Hill et al., 2004), was correlated with neuroticism and conscientiousness, whereas self-evaluative perfectionism was positively correlated with neuroticism and negatively correlated with agreeableness. Using the FMPS, personal standards and concern over mistakes were positively correlated with neuroticism (Egan et al., 2015). In a sample of Turkish college students using the APS-R, high standards were related to conscientiousness, openness, and extraversion, and discrepancy was related to neuroticism (Ulu & Tezer, 2010). Examining a large Dutch undergraduate sample, perfectionistic strivings were related to conscientiousness and both perfectionistic strivings and perfectionistic concerns had a negative relationship with emotional stability (DeCuyper et al., 2015). In contrast to research with adolescents, a few studies with undergraduates reported positive relationships between perfectionistic strivings and neuroticism, depending on the perfectionism measure.

Examining perfectionism and personality in adults has provided additional support for the connection between perfectionistic strivings-conscientiousness and the connection between perfectionistic concerns-neuroticism. Consistent with other research, perfectionistic strivings were associated with conscientiousness and perfectionistic concerns were associated with neuroticism in separate undergraduate and adult samples (Dunkley, Blankstein, & Berg, 2012). In addition, perfectionistic concerns were negatively associated with conscientiousness as were perfectionistic strivings negatively associated with neuroticism. These associations were likely due to using three perfectionism measures to create perfectionistic strivings and perfectionistic concerns (i.e., APS-R, FMPS,

HFMPS). The use of multiple measures also may have resulted in other significant correlations: perfectionistic strivings had positive associations with extraversion, whereas perfectionistic concerns had negative associations with agreeableness (Dunkley et al., 2012). Correlations between perfectionism and the five personality measures were similar between undergraduates and adults with one exception: perfectionistic strivings positively related to openness and perfectionistic concerns negatively related to openness only in the adult sample. In another study with adults, self-critical perfectionism from the Dysfunctional Attitude Scale (DAS; Weissman & Beck, 1978), was positively correlated with neuroticism and negatively correlated with extraversion, agreeableness, and conscientiousness (Dunkley & Kyperissis, 2008).

Across studies with different samples and different age groups, perfectionistic strivings were consistently associated with conscientiousness and perfectionistic concerns were associated with neuroticism. Individuals with the broad personality type of conscientiousness are likely to develop the narrow personality trait of perfectionistic strivings and individuals with general neurotic personalities are more likely to develop perfectionistic concerns. Unfortunately, we do not know the direction of this relationship. Do the broad, higher-order personality constructs influence lower-order personality traits or do lower-order personality traits influence higher-order personality constructs? There is only one longitudinal study that has specifically addressed this question. Conscientiousness at Time 1 predicted self-oriented perfectionism at Time 2 (about five to eight months apart), suggesting that elements of conscientiousness such as heightened attention to details and goal directed behaviors as broad, higher-level personality traits might be leading to the formation of narrow, lower-level personality traits such as perfectionism (Stoeber et al., 2009). However, neuroticism at Time 1 was not associated with increased self-oriented or socially prescribed perfectionism at Time 2. Unfortunately, the time frame of the study was only five to eight months and the data collected for Time 2 relied on adolescents returning their surveys by mail over the summer, resulting in a 62 percent return rate. Consequently, more longitudinal work is needed to determine the developmental pathways of association between broad, higher-order personality types and their relationships to lower-level, narrow personality traits such as perfectionism.

One open question involves whether dimensions of perfectionism contribute to psychological outcomes above and beyond broad personality constructs. In other words, are perfectionistic concerns simply a specific manifestation of neuroticism? Do perfectionistic strivings reflect a more specific type of conscientiousness? In short, the results are mixed: perfectionistic strivings and perfectionistic concerns contributed unique variance to the prediction of only certain outcomes after controlling for conscientiousness and neuroticism. For example, Rice et al. (2007) reported that when controlling for conscientiousness and neuroticism measures, concern over mistakes and discrepancy maintained negative relationships to self-esteem, whereas high standards maintained a positive relationship to self-esteem. However, other measures of perfectionistic strivings and perfectionistic concerns from the APS-R, HFMPS, and FMPS, with the exception of concern over mistakes, did not explain additional variance in predicting depression when controlling for conscientiousness and neuroticism (Rice et al., 2007). It should be noted that Rice et al. analyzed the subscales from the three perfectionism measures separately. When subscales from the APS-R, FMPS, and HFMPS were combined into measures of perfectionistic strivings (high standards, self-oriented, and personal standards) and perfectionistic concerns (discrepancy, socially prescribed, concern over mistakes), perfectionistic concerns contributed to the prediction of depressive and anxious symptoms after controlling for the Big Five personality constructs in undergraduates and adults (Dunkley et al., 2012). In a sample of middle-aged women, self-critical perfectionism (socially prescribed, concern over mistakes, and self-criticism subscales) at Time 1 predicted depressive symptoms at Time 2 after controlling for depressive symptoms and neuroticism at Time 1 (Sherry, Gautreau, Mushquash, Sherry, & Allen, 2014). Perfectionistic concerns conferred increased risk for low self-esteem and depressive symptoms beyond the broad personality construct of neuroticism.

Future Research on Big Five Personality Traits and Perfectionism in the Academic Context

To date, there has been no research that has examined interactions or moderating relationships among the Big Five personality constructs, perfectionism, and academic achievement. Perhaps the most obvious direction for future research on perfectionism, broad personality traits, and academic achievement will be to determine if perfectionistic strivings and perfectionistic concerns makes unique contributions to the prediction of academic outcomes such as GPA or exam scores after controlling for the effects of conscientiousness and neuroticism. Once researchers address the unique contribution of perfectionism, researchers should employ data analytic procedures to test potential moderating effects of perfectionism and Big Five personality traits. One can easily hypothesize that GPA may differ between students with perfectionistic strivings that have higher levels of conscientiousness compared to students with perfectionistic strivings that have lower levels of conscientiousness. In other words, interactions between perfectionistic strivings and conscientiousness and interactions between perfectionistic concerns and neuroticism should be included in statistical models.

In addition, broad personality constructs such as conscientiousness and neuroticism are associated with multiple narrow personality facets and predict different types of academic outcomes (McAbee, Oswald, & Connelly, 2014; Noftle & Robins, 2007). Some researchers have argued that the narrow facets provide a more nuanced picture of how personality predicts academic outcomes (see Paunonen & Ashton, 2013). Examining narrow facets of conscientiousness, MacCann, Duckworth, and Roberts (2009) found that different facets predicted different academic outcomes such as class absences, honors, and disciplinary reports in undergraduate students. Similarly, Rikoon et al. (2016) reported that narrow facets of conscientiousness had different prediction patterns with cognitive tests representing crystallized ability, fluid ability, quantitative reasoning, retrieval ability, and visual-spatial ability. Despite the wealth of work on broad constructs of personality and perfectionism, researchers have yet to examine how narrow facets might relate to perfectionistic strivings and perfectionistic concerns.

Perfectionistic concerns, a narrow personality trait, and the broad personality construct of neuroticism may both play a role in the imposter phenomenon—overwhelming feelings of being a fraud in ones' professional life, particularly among high-achievers (Vergauwe, Wille, Feys, De Fruyt, & Anseel, 2015). Examining professional, middle-aged Dutch workers, Vergauwe and colleagues (2015) reported that imposter tendencies were positively related to neuroticism, and in a separate regression analysis, were positively related to concern over mistakes and doubts about actions. The imposter phenomenon seems to have two components—high achievement and doubts about ones' intellectual ability—both of these parallel the two dimensions of perfectionistic strivings and perfectionistic concerns. Much more research is needed to determine the conceptual differences and similarities between imposter feelings and perfectionism and their consequences for higher education and workplace settings.

Summary

Perfectionistic concerns appear to be associated with a personal profile of insecure attachments with parents, behavioral tendencies toward approach-avoidance conflicts, and neuroticism. Perfectionistic strivings appear to be associated with a personal profile of approach/avoidance conflicts and conscientiousness. However, these conclusions are based almost exclusively on cross-sectional research with undergraduates and adults that have separately examined attachment or personality. Even within this cross-sectional research, to our knowledge, no research has focused on academic achievement. Longitudinal designs with children and adolescents, which incorporate measures of attachment, behavioral tendencies, and broad personality traits, will be necessary to fully understand how children and adolescents develop perfectionism and how perfectionism impacts academic achievement.

CHAPTER 3

Parenting and Perfectionism

Although longitudinal research must be conducted to determine the relationships among the factors that influence the development of perfectionism, the influence of parents on perfectionism has been widely examined (Appleton & Curran, 2016; Hewitt, Flett, & Mikail, 2017; Flett, Hewitt, Oliver, & Macdonald, 2002; Speirs Neumeister, 2004). Theoretical models of the development of perfectionism have mainly focused on environmental influences—how parents interact with their children. Yet children also inherit genetic traits from their parents. Research has revealed that perfectionism may have a genetic component, with higher correlations for perfectionism between identical twins compared to fraternal twins (Iranzo-Tatay et al., 2015; Tozzi et al., 2004). Genetic traits of both parents and their children impact the dynamics of their interactions, meaning that the development of perfectionistic traits results from genetic and environment interactions.

Empirical studies on parents have overwhelmingly drawn from the Flett et al. (2002) theoretical models that hypothesized different pathways from parenting to the development of children's perfectionism: the social expectations model, the social learning model, the social reactions model, and the anxious rearing model. The social expectations model and the social learning model have received the most attention in the research literature of parenting and perfectionism. Extending the review of Flett et al., we will use the four theoretical models to review recent research on parenting and perfectionism.

Social Expectations Model

The social expectations model hypothesized that parents who have extremely high, unrealistic expectations for their children's performance may lead to the development of perfectionism (Flett et al., 2002). Children may perceive that meeting these high parental expectations is the only way to gain parental approval. When parental approval is based on children's stellar performance, children may develop a sense of conditional self-worth meaning that self-esteem is contingent on meeting high parental expectations. Parental expectations are prominent in two widely used measures and conceptualizations of perfectionism. Frost and colleagues (Frost, Marten, Lahart, & Rosenblate, 1990) included two subscales related to parenting (parental expectations and parental criticism) in the Frost Multidimensional Perfectionism Scale (FMPS). Socially prescribed perfectionism, the belief that one perceives that other important people expect him/her to be perfect, is directly related to parents' expectations for perfection. Specific items on the Hewitt and Flett Multidimensional Perfectionism Scale (HFMPS; Hewitt & Flett, 1991) ask individuals to rate how much they agree that their parents expect them to be perfect. Although researchers have recently argued that parental expectations and parental criticism are antecedents of perfectionism rather than defining features (Shafran & Mansell, 2001; Rice, Lopez, & Vergara, 2005; Stoeber & Otto, 2006), parental expectations and parental criticism are prominent features in defining and explaining perfectionism.

Much of the research on parenting and perfectionism has focused on the role of parental expectations and parental criticism, or how parents react to children's failure to live up to parents' high expectations. According to Flett et al. (2002), parental expectations may range from unrealistic expectations for children's perfection to expectations for children's low achievement or even failure. This range of parental expectations and its impact on perfectionism are central in the social expectations model. However, parental expectations conceptually overlap with levels of parental criticism, which may range from constructive criticism about children's performance to harsh, demeaning personal attacks about children's performance. Harsh and demeaning family environments are prominent in the social reactions model. Flett et al. discussed the overlap between the social expectations and social reactions model. For our purposes, we will review the research literature on parental expectations and parental criticism to examine the social expectations model and studies focused on parental warmth and control will be reviewed for the social reactions model.

Research with children and adolescents has supported the link between high parental expectations and high parental criticism and perfectionistic concerns. Hutchinson and Yates (2008) examined mother–adolescent dyads on the Magill Perfectionism Scale (i.e., selected subscales from the Child and Adolescent Perfectionism Scale (CAPS) consisting of self-striving, socially prescribed, and concern over mistakes) and different types of parents' goals for their children. Parents' direct expectations (i.e., setting high standards for their child) were related to perfectionistic strivings and negatively related to perfectionistic concerns. Controlling parental expectations (i.e., expressing disappointment and extremely high importance on meeting high standards), which are similar to parental criticism, were positively associated with perfectionistic concerns. Using the FMPS with a sample of elite adolescent athletes, personal standards were positively related to parental expectations whereas concern over mistakes were related to parental criticism (McArdle & Duda, 2008). In short, parents setting high expectations for their children might result in the development of perfectionistic strivings, whereas parents' negative reactions to their children not meeting their standards may lead to perfectionistic concerns.

In one of the few studies to employ a multidimensional, person-centered analysis, McArdle and Duda (2004) examined 12- to 17-year-old elite athletes on perfectionism and perceptions about their parents' expectations and criticism. In addition, athletes were surveyed about their perceptions of their parents' goals for their sports performance and their goals for their own performance. Adolescent and parent goals were classified as having an ego goal orientation (i.e., focused on normative comparisons and display of superior ability) or a task goal orientation (i.e., focused on personal improvement and learning). Using cluster analysis, four different clusters were found: ego-involving/structured environment, high ability focused (highest parental ego orientation)/flexible environment, task-involving/flexible environment, and punitive (highest parental expectations and criticism)/structured environment. Clusters with structured environments received low scores on the Family Adaptability and Cohesion Scale II (Olson, Portner, & Bell, 1982) meaning that the adolescent athletes perceived that their families were rigid in control and discipline. In contrast, flexible environment clusters had high scores on the Family Adaptability and Cohesion Scale II (Olson et al., 1982) indicating that adolescent athletes perceived that their families had a more democratic type of climate surrounding rules and control. Athletes in the high ability focused/flexible environment and the punitive/structured environment reported higher levels of parental expectations and parental criticism than athletes in the other two groups. When examining differences across groups, athletes in the high ability focused/flexible environment and the punitive/structured environment also had significantly higher concern over mistakes subscale scores than the athletes in the other two groups. Adolescent athletes in each group were similar in their levels of personal standards. In the context of sports, parental expectations and parental criticism were associated with perfectionistic concerns but not perfectionistic strivings. Given that adolescents in this study were national competitors in various sports, this sample of adolescents was selective and had likely internalized high levels of perfectionistic strivings, with only variability existing in perfectionistic concerns.

Future Research on the Social Expectations Model in the Academic Context

In order to fully understand parental expectations and parental criticism as precursors to perfectionism, longitudinal research is needed. Only one longitudinal study related to perfectionism and parental expectations and parental criticism was found. In a large sample of 15- to 19-year-old Romanian adolescents, self-oriented perfectionism correlated with perceptions of parental expectations but not parental criticism and socially prescribed perfectionism correlated with perceptions of parental expectations and parental criticism (Damian, Stoeber, Negru, & Baban, 2013). Adolescents who reported that their parents had high expectations at Time 1 had higher levels of socially prescribed perfectionism at Time 2 (i.e., seven to nine months later than Time 1). Parental criticism did not predict longitudinal increases in either self-oriented perfectionism or socially prescribed perfectionism. Results for this longitudinal study are inconsistent with hypothesized predictions about the role of parental criticism in the development of perfectionistic concerns. Much more longitudinal research is needed to determine the specific developmental pathways among parental expectations, parental criticism, and different types of perfectionism.

Within future longitudinal research, researchers are also encouraged to include measures of children's willingness to internalize parental values and goals (Tong & Lam, 2011). As Flett et al. (2002) hypothesized, children's willingness to internalize parents' expectations as their own may play an important role in the development of perfectionism. Children's willingness to internalize parents' expectations may also be influenced by how closely those expectations for children's achievement actually match their children's competence. Researchers have speculated that aspects of competence and motivation might underlie individuals' perfectionistic tendencies in certain domains (Dunn, Dunn, & McDonald, 2012; Flett et al., 2002; Hall, 2016; McArdle, 2010). It seems plausible that parents focus their exceedingly high expectations and demands for perfect performance on those domains in which their children may show superior abilities (Appleton & Curran, 2016; Flett et al., 2002). Thus, an open research question is whether parents' expectations for their children actually *match* their children's level of ability in the academic domain. Furthermore, when parents' expectations do match their children's abilities, are children more likely to internalize their parents' perfectionistic expectations as their own? One can easily hypothesize that children with superior intellectual ability would view their parents' high standards for their academic achievement as valid. Parental expectations perceived by children as valid and appropriate might be more easily internalized. In contrast, children with moderate levels of intellectual ability may question parents' expectations for exceedingly high academic achievement that, in their perceptions, seem out of reach and impossible. To our knowledge, no perfectionism research has examined the connections among parental expectations, children's competence, or the match between the two constructs.

Social Learning Model

Parents' tendencies to set extremely high standards of performance and being hypercritical when those standards are not met may be an outward reflection of parents' own perfectionism. According to the theory of social development of Alfred Bandura, children observe other people in their environment and imitate their behaviors, particularly if children view those people as powerful, caring, and competent (Bandura, 1977, 1986). Children may observe parents who strive for perfection and/or have negative reactions to their mistakes and failures and adopt these perfectionistic behaviors. The notion that parents' perfectionism may facilitate the development of perfectionism has theoretical consistency with two of the developmental models outlined by Flett and his colleagues (2002): social expectations and social learning. In the social expectations model, Flett and colleagues postulated that perfectionism develops in response to parental approval that is contingent upon children's performance. Contingent approval may be indicative of parents exhibiting high levels of other-oriented perfectionism, leading to unrealistic expectations for their children. Contingent approval may also stem from parents' high levels of either self-oriented or socially prescribed perfectionism as they may pressure themselves or feel pressure from others to produce perfect children. Consequently, children experiencing such contingent approval may develop a sense of helplessness if they fail to meet their parents' expectations. Such conditional self-worth, a central component of perfectionistic concerns, is likely to develop in children and adolescents. The social learning model emphasizes the tendency for children to model perfectionistic behaviors that they observe from their parents. Overall, research exploring parent and child perfectionism offers support for these two developmental models, but the findings suggest a complex relationship in need of further elucidation.

Research supports correlations between parents' measures of perfectionism and their children's measures of perfectionism (Frost, Lahart, & Rosenblate, 1991; Vieth & Trull, 1999). Moreover, there is a trend in the direct of significant correlations between children's perfectionism and the perfectionism of the same-sex parent as opposed to the opposite sex parent (Frost et al., 1991; Vieth & Trull, 1999). The majority of the research on parents' and children's levels of perfectionism has relied on children's perceptions of their parents' perfectionism rather than parents' actual self-reporting of perfectionism. For example, in a qualitative study of gifted high school students, Speirs Neumeister, Williams, and Cross (2009) found that participants scoring high on one or more of self-oriented, socially prescribed, or other-oriented perfectionism perceived their parents as exhibiting perfectionistic behaviors such as maintaining unrealistic expectations for their children, and yelling, threatening, or ridiculing their children when their parents' high expectations were not met. The participants attributed their own perfectionism as developing in part in response to observing the perfectionistic tendencies of their parents and internalizing them as their own.

Other studies of gifted students at different developmental levels report similar findings. Speirs Neumeister (2004) found that when college-aged participants scoring high on both self-oriented and socially prescribed perfectionism were asked what contributed to the development of their perfectionism, they said that the observance of their parents' perfectionist behaviors was a central factor. Additionally, in a study examining perfectionism in middle-school gifted students, Siegle and Schuler (2000) found that gifted first-born students or gifted male students reported parents as having high expectations for their performance.

Although these studies suggest a relationship between children's perfectionism and parents' perfectionism, the researchers did not directly measure parental perfectionism. Thus, it may be the children's *perception of their parents' perfectionism*, rather than the parents' actual level of perfectionism, that may be correlated with children's level of perfectionism. Appleton, Hall, and Hill (2010) addressed this question directly in an examination of elite junior athletes and their parents. Athletes' perceptions of parents' self-oriented perfectionism predicted athletes' self-oriented perfectionism, and athletes' perception of parents' other-oriented perfectionism predicted athletes' other-oriented perfectionism. Athletes' perceptions of both their parents' socially prescribed and other-oriented perfectionism significantly predicted athletes' socially prescribed perfectionism. Perhaps most importantly, parents' self-reported perfectionism did not predict athletes' perfectionism, suggesting the importance of children's perceptions of parents' perfectionism for understanding the development of perfectionism.

Similarly, parents' self-reported perfectionism has had little significance in predicting children's perfectionism in other studies. For example, Clark and Coker (2009) found no correlation between 11- to 15-year-old adolescents' perfectionistic concerns and their mothers' perfectionistic concerns. Parental self-reported self-oriented or socially prescribed perfectionism did not predict adolescents' self-oriented perfectionism, as measured by the Child and Adolescent Perfectionism Scale, in fathers and daughters (Cook & Kearney, 2009). Mothers' self-oriented and socially prescribed perfectionism predicted sons' self-oriented perfectionism and maternal obsessive-compulsive symptoms were found to mediate the relationship between mothers' self-oriented perfectionism and sons' self-oriented perfectionism.

Future Research on the Social Learning Model in the Academic Context

Collectively, the studies that have examined parent perfectionism and child perfectionism highlight future areas of research needed to better understand the complexity of this relationship. Further clarification is needed in the measurement of parent and child perfectionism. Measuring children's perception of parental perfectionism may be more significant than the parents' self-reported perfectionism in predicting children's perfectionism. Perhaps children who exhibit perfectionism are more likely to perceive their parents as perfectionistic even if their parents do not self-report the same high levels of perfectionism. Inversely, parents with high levels of actual perfectionism may not be willing to rate themselves as such in order to portray a more positive self-image. However, to date, no study was found that included objective measures of child and parent perfectionism. To the extent that observational studies could be designed to include third party objective raters of parent and child perfectionism, the predictive relationship between parents' and their children's perfectionism may be better understood.

In addition to clarifying the methods of measuring perfectionism in parents and children, the introduction of more complex prediction models may also help explain this relationship. The studies reviewed indicated that parent and child gender and/or primary caregiver status may uniquely predict perfectionism in children (Appleton et al., 2010; Cook & Kearney, 2009; 2014). Likewise, the predictive significance of parents' perfectionism on the development of their children's perfectionism may vary according to the developmental age of the child (e.g., Cook & Kearney,

2014), thereby calling for the need to systematically evaluate this relationship using longitudinal designs. Finally, the typicality of the sample also needs to be considered when evaluating the results. Several studies examined academically gifted students (e.g., Speirs Neumeister, 2004; Speirs Neumeister et al., 2009) or elite junior athletes (Appleton et al., 2010). Perhaps highly talented youth differentially interpret their parents' perfectionism compared with typical children and adolescents, thereby negating the comparison of findings across studies. Studies including both typical and atypical (e.g., academically, athletically, or artistically gifted) youth and their parents are needed. The results of such future studies will clarify the relationship between parent and child perfectionism as well as support or weaken the social learning model of perfectionism (Flett et al., 2002).

Social Reactions Model

The social expectations model and the social learning model are similar in the focus on variability in somewhat typical aspects of parenting: having goals and aspirations for your children, offering feedback about your children's behavior, and modeling behaviors. Yet parents may differ in how they engage in these typical socialization practices with their children in emotional tone, ranging from a warm and caring manner to a harsh and punitive manner. For example, Hamachek (1978) posited that unhealthy perfectionism develops in family environments when parental love and approval are perceived as conditional based on performance. When parental behaviors involve manipulative tactics of asserting authority (i.e., authoritarian parenting), withdrawal of love, and/or guilt induction (i.e., psychological control) applied in an uncaring manner, children and adolescents may view their family life as harsh and chaotic. Children may adopt being perfect as a way to reduce the likelihood of harsh criticism or loss of affection from parents. Parental criticism and parental expectations are also involved in the social expectations model; however, Flett et al. (2002) differentiated the two models based on the parenting dimension of responsiveness: the extent to which parents react and interact in a warm and caring manner toward their children.

Flett and colleagues (2002) drew from a prominent model of parenting in developmental psychology that proposed that different levels of responsiveness and demandingness (i.e., the extent to which parents demand compliance and supervise their children's behaviors) predicted different psychological and achievement outcomes for children and adolescents. Parenting styles were initially explained in Baumrind's (1971) standard typology and Maccoby and Martin's (1983) revised model. According to Baumrind, styles of parenting can be characterized across two dimensions: demandingness and responsiveness. Based on these two characteristics, Baumrind identified three parental styles: authoritarian, authoritative, and permissive. In a later extension of the model, Maccoby and Martin (1983) further divided the permissive style to create a fourth style: neglectful.

In this typology, Baumrind (1971) portrayed authoritarian parenting as demonstrating high levels of demandingness coupled with low levels of responsiveness. These parents were focused on controlling their children, including their children's behaviors and attitudes, and these parents demanded obedience and respect for authority. Typically, obedience and respect for authority were demanded with little concern for the children's feelings and opinions. In contrast, Baumrind described authoritative parents as those with both high levels of demandingness and high levels of responsiveness. While these parents monitored their children's behavior, they used non-punitive forms of discipline when standards for behavior were not met. Authoritative parents both appreciated their children's points of view when establishing rules and were warm and caring toward their children.

A third style of parenting, permissive, resulted when parents showed low levels of demandingness and high levels of responsiveness. Similar to authoritative parents, permissive parents demonstrated warm and accepting attitudes toward their children; however, they also exhibited a lack of control over their children (Baumrind, 1971). Finally, low levels of both demandingness and responsiveness were characteristic of neglectful parents. Neglectful parents did not offer their children any support or attention. They did not attempt to control their children's behaviors but rather remained uninvolved in their children's lives (Maccoby & Martin, 1983).

Studies have examined the relationship between parenting styles and various indices of perfectionism. Only a few studies have examined the role of permissive and neglectful parenting styles on perfectionism.

Predominately, researchers have focused on the potential role that authoritative parenting may play in the development of perfectionistic strivings and the role that authoritarian parenting may play in the development of perfectionistic concerns.

Parenting Styles and Perfectionism

The influence of mothers and fathers' authoritarian parenting on perfectionism has been investigated extensively in numerous studies with participants from multiple cultures, age groups, gender, and gifted/non-gifted ability levels. Additionally, studies have examined perfectionism as a general trait and as a specific trait in particular domains such as sports. Results from these studies revealed several consistent patterns as well as subtle differences in relationships between authoritarian parenting and perfectionism depending on participant characteristics.

The majority of the studies across two decades of research have reported that authoritarian parenting predicted perfectionistic concerns. In support of this theory, harsh parenting, as measured by the Critical Parenting Inventory (Randolph & Dykman, 1996), significantly predicted perfectionistic concerns (Enns, Cox, & Clara, 2002). Moreover, in this study, students' perfectionistic concerns fully mediated the relationship between harsh parenting and students' depressive symptoms. As such, understanding the dynamics of parenting that lead to perfectionistic concerns is critical, particularly in children and adolescents.

Using the HFMPS, socially prescribed perfectionism in undergraduates was related to authoritarian parenting for males (Flett, Hewitt, & Singer, 1995). Rice, Ashby, and Preusser (1996) found that undergraduates classified as neurotic perfectionists, with high scores on the high standards and organization subscale of the Almost Perfect Scale (APS; Slaney & Johnson, 1992) coupled with high scores on the FMPS subscale of concern over mistakes, reported that their parents exhibited more authoritarian characteristics than the parents of undergraduates classified as normal perfectionists (i.e., high scores on the high standards and organization subscale of the APS and low scores on FMPS subscale concern over mistakes). Hibbard and Walton (2014) also found that authoritarian parenting was associated with higher scores on the FMPS subscales of parental expectations, parental criticism, and doubts about actions for females and male undergraduate students. But for males only, authoritarian parenting also was associated with higher scores for concerns over mistakes. Finally, Gong, Fletcher, and Bolin (2015) found that maternal authoritarian parenting was positively associated with concern over mistakes and doubts about actions for male and female undergraduate students.

Studies of academically able students also support the relationship between authoritarian parenting and perfectionistic concerns. In two studies of academically able undergraduates (Miller, Lambert, & Speirs Neumeister, 2012; Speirs Neumeister, 2004), participants that scored high on socially prescribed perfectionism viewed one or both of their parents as authoritarian. Maternal and paternal authoritarian parenting predicted perfectionistic concerns, as measured by the FMPS subscales of concern over mistakes, parental expectations, parental criticism, and doubts about actions, in a study of gifted, high school Malaysian students (Basirion, Majid, & Jelas, 2014).

Finally, researchers also have investigated potential cross-cultural differences on the influence of authoritarian parenting on perfectionistic concerns. Using an Australian sample of undergraduates and an Australian version of the FMPS (Khawaja & Armstrong, 2005), Craddock, Church, and Sands (2009) found that perfectionistic concerns predicted authoritarian parenting. In a study comparing Asian-American with Caucasian-American undergraduates, Kawamura, Frost, and Harmatz (2002) investigated the relationship between authoritarian and psychologically controlling parenting and mixed perfectionism, as defined by three subscales from the FMPS: concern over mistakes, doubts about actions, and personal standards. Asian-American students rated both their parents as harsh and more authoritarian than did Caucasian students. Moreover, Asian-Americans scored higher for perfectionistic concerns, but not perfectionistic strivings, compared to Caucasians. But after controlling for parenting variables, ethnicity did not predict differences in perfectionism. Additionally, for Asian-Americans, the correlations between paternal harshness-concern over mistakes and paternal authoritarianism-doubts about actions were significant only for Asian-American females, but not males.

Collectively, research supports the relationship between authoritarian parenting and perfectionistic concerns. A surprising finding in some studies, however, is the relationship between authoritarian parenting and perfectionistic strivings. For example, Gong et al. (2015) found that authoritarian parenting was associated with high scores on the personal standards subscale of the FMPS and Craddock et al. (2009) found that perfectionistic strivings, also defined by the FMPS subscales, was predicted by authoritarian parenting. One potential reason for the unexpected relationship between authoritarian parenting and perfectionistic strivings may be attributed to how parenting styles were operationalized in the two studies: Gong et al. only examined maternal parenting styles and Craddock et al. collapsed maternal and paternal ratings into an average parenting style rating. Furthermore, neither study included a separate measure of maternal and paternal styles or an indicator of what parent the participant represented as the primary caregiver. These constraints preclude a full analysis of the influence of authoritarian parenting on perfectionistic strivings. Moreover, perfectionistic strivings have been hypothesized to have stronger associations with authoritative parenting than authoritarian parenting.

Examining the role of authoritative parenting on perfectionism, studies have suggested a positive relationship between authoritative parenting and perfectionistic strivings. Self-oriented perfectionism was related to authoritative parenting but only for females (Flett et al., 1995). Two studies investigating parenting styles and perfectionism in academically able students also found relationships between authoritative parenting and perfectionistic strivings (Miller et al., 2012; Speirs Neumeister, 2004). Basirion et al. (2014) found that authoritative parenting predicted personal standards and organization as measured by the FMPS. Similarly, in the domain of sports using the Sport-MSP-2 (Gotwals & Dunn, 2009), Sapieja, Dunn, and Holt (2011) reported that healthy perfectionists (i.e., high personal standards and medium levels of concern over mistakes, parental pressure, coach pressure, and doubts about actions) and non-perfectionists had higher perceptions of both maternal and paternal authoritativeness than unhealthy perfectionists (i.e., higher scores on personal standards, concern over mistakes, parental pressure, coach pressure, doubts about actions). One study did not show a relationship between authoritative parenting and perfectionistic strivings, as measured by personal standards and organization from the FMPS (Hibbard & Walton, 2014). However, Hibbard and Walton (2014) used a shorter, modified version of the Parental Authority Questionnaire (Buri, 1991) and reports for mothers and fathers were combined into one parenting style score, possibly accounting for the inconsistent results.

Using this adapted version of the Parental Authority Questionnaire (Buri, 1991), Hibbard and Walton (2014) examined the relationship of perfectionism and the other two parenting styles: indulgent (permissive) and neglectful parenting. Indulgent parenting was negatively related to parental criticism for both sexes, and negatively related to concern over mistakes for males only. Neglectful parenting was positively associated with parental criticism for both males and females. Neglectful parenting was positively associated with the doubts about actions for males and negatively associated with organization for females. Although much more work is needed regarding how these two parenting styles are related to perfectionism, indulgent (permissive) parenting may act as a buffer against the development of perfectionistic concerns, whereas neglectful parenting may foster the development of perfectionistic concerns (Hibbard & Walton, 2014).

Parental Psychological Control and Perfectionism

Whereas there has been a wealth of research devoted to parenting styles and perfectionism, researchers have only recently begun to try to tease apart how specific parenting practices might uniquely contribute to perfectionism. One such parenting practice, psychological control, has been implicated in the development of perfectionistic concerns. Parental psychological control is characterized by the use of coercive techniques such as guilt trips and withholding affection in order to gain children's compliance (Barber, 1996; Schaefer, 1965). Such coercive parenting tactics are attempts to control children's psychological or internal feelings, thoughts, and goals, and are likely to frustrate children's and adolescents' autonomy because of pressure to think, act, and feel how the parent wants (Soenens & Vansteenkiste, 2010). With regard to perfectionism, parental psychological control would fit within the social expectations model. That is, children who do not adopt their parents' exceedingly high standards and strive to meet those standards risk losing their parents' affection. In addition, they are made to feel guilty when they fail to live up to perfectionistic standards. When this occurs, children's internalization of parents' expectations for perfection, either fully or partially, may be an adaptive strategy to avoid parental rejection and disapproval. In more extreme cases, if the nature of parents' psychological manipulation is excessively cruel, then children may develop perfectionism as a coping mechanism within this harsh environment, consistent with the social reactions model.

Does parental psychological control influence children's perfectionistic traits beyond authoritarian parenting? In one of the few studies that examined parenting styles and parental psychological control, authoritarian parenting was associated with perfectionistic strivings and perfectionistic concerns, but only perfectionistic concerns were associated with psychologically controlling parenting (Craddock et al., 2009). Similar to the findings of Craddock et al. (2009), other researchers have found that psychologically controlling parenting was associated with perfectionistic concerns (Fletcher, Shim, & Wang, 2012; Shih, 2013; Soenens et al., 2005, 2008), with only one study reporting a positive relationship between personal standards and parental psychological control (Gong, Paulson, & Wang, 2016). However, this work has mainly examined undergraduate students. Undergraduate students are typically away from home and have little or no direct, face-to-face contact with their parents on a daily basis. Although undergraduates still interact with parents, most of them are not "under their roof" and subject to their direct control. As such, research findings based on undergraduate students may not generalize to children and adolescents who interact with their parents on a daily basis.

Because of this, research that has examined children and adolescents are more likely to demonstrate the relationship between parental psychological control and children's perfectionism. In one of the few studies with children, mothers were asked to work with their 10-year-old children on a challenging task (Kenney-Benson & Pomerantz, 2005). Mothers' levels of controlling behaviors toward their children when they worked on the challenging task predicted children's perfectionistic concerns, and in turn, perfectionistic concerns mediated the relationship between maternal control and children's depressive symptoms. In a sample of eighth grade Taiwanese students, Shih (2013) reported that parental psychological control predicted students' concern over mistakes and doubts about actions. Using a longitudinal design, Soenens and colleagues (2008) collected data from 15- to 18-year-old adolescents about perceived parents' psychological control, adolescents' perfectionism, and depressive symptoms at Time 1. Mothers and fathers' self-reported use of psychologically controlling techniques were also collected at Time 1. For the next two years, data were collected from adolescents on perfectionism after one year (Time 2) and depressive symptoms after two years (Time 3). Controlling for adolescents' perfectionistic concerns at Time 1, parental psychological control at Time 1 predicted adolescents' perfectionistic concerns one year later, and, in turn, adolescents' perfectionistic concerns predicted depressive symptoms two years later. In other words, adolescents' perfectionistic concerns served as a mediator for the long-term relationship between parental psychological control and adolescents' depressive symptoms. In a sample of 7-year-old children followed until age 11, Hong et al. (2016) reported that parental intrusiveness, as measured by coding parents' controlling behavior in a parent–child interaction task, predicted increasing levels of self-critical perfectionism. The longitudinal design, multiple informants, and behavioral measures of psychologically controlling parenting strengthen conclusions from these studies about the role of parental psychological control in the development of perfectionistic concerns.

Although psychological controlling parenting is aimed at obtaining children's compliance with demands and expectations, there is some evidence that parents may adopt psychological control with their children in the service of different types of goals. Soenens and colleagues (Soenens, Vansteenkiste, & Luyten, 2010) have proposed a conceptual framework and established a measure for achievement-oriented psychological control and dependency-oriented psychological control. According to Soenens et al. (2010), parents focused on their children's achievement use psychological control to obtain their children's compliance to meet their achievement expectations. In contrast, parents who are focused on maintaining emotional closeness and encouraging their children's dependency on them use psychological control to maintain their children's enmeshment in the family. Dependency-oriented psychological control was related to another measure of family enmeshment, whereas achievement-oriented psychological control was associated with undergraduate students' perceptions of a perfectionistic family climate (i.e., FMPS parental expectations and parental criticism subscales). Moreover, parents' own perfectionistic concerns were related to achievement-oriented psychological control but not dependency-oriented psychological control. Dependency-oriented psychological control predicted adolescents' reported dependency on their parents and achievement-oriented psychological control predicted adolescents' self-criticism (Soenens et al., 2010).

Given that parental psychological control predicted perfectionistic concerns, additional research is needed to identify those parents who might be most likely to use psychologically coercive parenting practices. In a sample of female Dutch undergraduate students and their mothers and fathers, parents' perfectionistic concerns and parents' neuroticism predicted parents' use of psychological control. Moreover, parents' psychological control mediated the relationship between parents' perfectionistic concerns and their daughters' perfectionistic concerns (Soenens et al., 2005). Consistent with these findings, Bleys et al. (2016) found that parental self-criticism predicted parents' use of achievement-oriented psychological control with their adolescents. In other words, parents who are self-critical adopt parenting styles that express criticism and disappointment when children fail to meet parental expectations (Bleys et al., 2016). In a sample of elite adolescent gymnasts and soccer players, parents' empathy partially mediated parental psychological control and parents' socially prescribed perfectionism, meaning that parents are focused on their own needs for perfection and are unable to empathize with the needs of their children (Appleton & Curran, 2016).

Future Research on the Social Reactions Model and Perfectionism in the Academic Context

Harsh, intrusive, and psychologically manipulative parenting seems to be an antecedent for the development of perfectionistic concerns (Hong et al., 2016; Soenens et al., 2008). And although more longitudinal work is needed, authoritative parenting may be a precursor to the development of perfectionistic strivings. However, we know little about how permissive or neglectful parenting might influence the development of perfectionism. The parenting dimension common to permissive parenting and neglectful parenting is lack of demandingness and boundary setting for children's mature behavior and compliance. Without rules and boundaries to guide children's behavior, families with permissive or neglectful parents may seem chaotic and unstructured. As such, children may be left to figure out their own boundaries and rules for appropriate behavior. According to Flett et al. (2002), adopting perfectionistic traits may be a way for some children to gain control of their lives within the context of a chaotic household. To our knowledge, only one study has been conducted with a sample of maltreated adolescents (Flett, Druckman, Hewitt, & Wekerle, 2012). Future research on parenting and perfectionism must include families from different levels of dysfunction to fully test the social reactions model.

Anxious Rearing Model

Authoritarian parents and psychologically controlling parents use manipulative techniques to squelch their children's autonomy, pushing their children to adopt and approach their parents' desired expectations. Controlling parents might be focused on the positive outcomes that parents believe will be achieved with their children's perfect performance such as scholarships, awards, and praise from others. In contrast, anxious rearing parents are focused on the potential negative consequences of pursuing high personal goals, such as imagined threats and judgments from others, that might lead to parental overprotection (Flett et al., 2002; Appleton & Curran, 2016). In the anxious rearing model, anxious parents who are focused on mistakes and negative consequences of mistakes may impart anxiety in their children surrounding failure and making mistakes. Parents who are hyperfocused on threats and judgments from others might become overprotective. Parental overprotection may increase children's tendencies to avoid novel situations and evaluative situations due to fear of negative consequences.

In one of the few studies that specifically investigated the anxious rearing model, Mitchell, Broeren, Newall, and Hudson (2013) experimentally manipulated the behavior of parents (high perfectionistic rearing behaviors vs. non-perfectionistic rearing behaviors) when working with their 7- to 12-year-old children (i.e., about half non-anxious and half clinically anxious) during a copy task. Children then completed the copy task alone and their perfectionistic behaviors were coded. Results showed that all children in the "high perfectionistic rearing behaviors" group increased in their observed perfectionistic behaviors at the second copy tasks (Mitchell et al., 2013). This experimental study provides evidence that parents' enhanced messages about mistakes and failures impact perfectionistic behavior and represents one of the only studies strictly devoted to investigating the anxious rearing model.

Although there has been little research devoted specifically to the anxious rearing model (Appleton & Curran, 2016; Flett et al., 2002), a few studies suggest that parents' perfectionism may be related to parental anxiety, leading to overprotective parenting. Overly anxious parents may hover and overcontrol their children's behaviors in attempts to prevent their children from mistakes and failure, sending the message to their children that mistakes and failure are to be avoided at all costs. In a sample of 8- to 12-year-old children, Cook and Kearney (2014) found that maternal anxiety mediated the relationship between maternal other-oriented perfectionism and children's socially prescribed perfectionism. Affrunti and Woodruff-Borden (2015) reported that parent perfectionism mediated the relationship between parental anxiety and parental overcontrol, as measured from a parent–child interaction task, in a sample of children diagnosed with anxiety disorder.

Parental overcontrol beyond the childhood years, however, may be especially problematic. During late adolescents and early adulthood, an extreme form of parental control, helicopter parenting, has received some research attention. Helicopter parenting refers to overprotective and over-involved parenting and appears to be an overlapping, but distinct type of parental control (Padilla-Walker & Nelson, 2012). Using confirmatory factor analysis, Padilla-Walker and Nelson (2012) found that helicopter parenting items represented a distinct construct from behavioral control and psychological control parenting items. Items related to helicopter parenting seemed to represent an active form of control involving others (e.g., intervenes in setting disputes with my roommates and friends), whereas psychological and behavioral control items were more focused on controlling the child. Similar to psychologically controlling parenting, helicopter parenting had a negative relationship with parenting autonomy granting (Schiffrin et al., 2014). Padilla-Walker and Nelson stated that parents use these practices, "out of strong parental concern for the well-being and success of the child" (p. 1186). It is not a stretch to see how helicopter parenting might influence students' perfectionistic traits. However, to date, there has been no published research on helicopter parenting and perfectionism.

Future Research on the Anxious Rearing Model and Perfectionism in the Academic Context

There has been little research attention or support for the anxious rearing model (Appleton & Curran, 2016; Flett et al., 2002; Speirs Neumeister et al., 2009). In short, anxious rearing parents are hard to identify with survey methods. Observational methods (Affrunti & Woodruff-Borden, 2015; Hong et al., 2016; Kenney-Benson & Pomerantz, 2005) and fine-grained analyses of the content of parent messages that highlight the negative consequences of imperfection to their children, similar to the methods used by Mitchell et al. (2013), will be necessary. Future researchers will need to determine a way to identify such messages, through qualitative research or conversation analysis, to identify and study anxious rearing parenting.

Summary

To examine any constructs related to parenting, future research must utilize samples of children and adolescents and move away from examining undergraduate students. Studies with college students necessitate a retrospective, self-report measure of any parenting construct instead of a real-time assessment. To minimize the potential inaccuracies of retrospective reporting of perceived parenting, more research is needed with children and adolescents who are currently living with a parent or both parents. When children are living with both parents, it will be important to analyze paternal and maternal parenting scores separately and to determine the parent who is the primary caregiver. Likewise, children's perceptions of parenting are particularly relevant for predicting perfectionistic traits (Appleton & Curran, 2016; Appleton et al., 2010). Thus, data on parents' self-report of their own parenting and their children's perceptions of their parenting is necessary. Additionally, clearer operational definitions of parenting will also provide a more detailed understanding of the relationship of parenting to perfectionism. For example, by examining styles and practices, Craddock et al. (2009) reported different types of perfectionism had differential relationships to authoritarian parenting and psychological control. Psychologically controlling parenting encompasses specific parental behaviors (guilt trip, withholding affection), whereas parenting styles represent more general ways that parents interact with their children. Although studies with children and adolescents may provide more accurate data, these studies will not address how parenting impacts the development of perfectionism. Research questions about the development of perfectionism require developmental research methods. Only long-term, longitudinal studies will fully address the developmental pathways related to parenting and children's perfectionism.

CHAPTER 4

Achievement Motivation and Perfectionism

In the field of sports psychology, there has been a long history of research on how perfectionism influences motivational processes for athletic training and performance (Flett & Hewitt, 2005; Gaudreau & Antl, 2008; Hall, 2016; Hall, Kerr, & Mathews, 1998; Stoeber, 2011, 2014). Elite and competitive athletes have been the focus of this research because perfectionism has been thought to manifest in individuals having perceived competence for a specific skill (Flett, Hewitt, Oliver, & Macdonald, 2002) that is personally relevant and important (Dunn, Causgrove Dunn, & McDonald, 2012; Hall, 2016; Shafran, Cooper, & Fairburn, 2002). Elite athletes have superior competence and their commitment to a particular sport is part of their identity, meaning that they are highly motivated to adhere to rigorous training schedules in order to achieve optimal performance.

How does perfectionism and motivation in the sports domain compare to perfectionism and motivation in the academic domain? Perfectionism and motivation in the sports and academic domain are similar in that adolescence and emerging adulthood are the developmental years that are typically devoted to athletic and academic pursuits. Academic and athletic pursuits expand adolescents' and young adults' beliefs about their competence and achievement. Competence in academic and athletic domains also becomes integrated into a coherent sense of self, identity, and personality during these developmental years.

Despite these similarities, we argue that there are at least two fundamental differences between the two domains that impact research findings on perfectionism and motivation. First, in most sports, athletes' performances are evaluated on personal or team records, self-reflection, and feedback from coaches, parents, and others. Some exceptions include sports such as diving, figure skating, and gymnastics where expert judges evaluate athletes' performances. For most sports, however, there is no perfect score and athletic performance can always be improved. For students in academic settings, there is a perfect score (100 percent) for most school grading systems and a maximum score on standardized assessments. Thus, students with perfectionism may be under the impression that *perfection is possible* for their academic performance. Second, elite athletes in competitive sports represent a selective sample of individuals who were chosen for the sport or team based on their abilities and talents. Athletes in competitive sports are also committed to grueling training and competition schedules, suggesting high levels of motivation for the sport. Children and adolescents in most industrialized countries are required by law to attend public schools and only some private schools have student selection processes. Because participation in academic settings is mandatory as opposed to voluntary, students' motivation may be compromised. It has been estimated that more than one-third of high school students in the United States are disengaged from their academic studies (National Research Council, 2004). Considering this statistic, improving students' motivation has been suggested as a crucial part of school reform (Usher & Kober, 2012). How might students' achievement motivation be influenced by perfectionism? Stoeber, Damian, and Madigan (2017) have recently argued that examining the different motivational profiles associated with perfectionistic strivings and perfectionistic concerns may be the key to understanding why perfectionism may be related to both positive and negative achievement outcomes. Whereas Stoeber and colleagues have published an exhaustive review of perfectionism and motivation across domains, we have selected to review only research on perfectionism and achievement motivation in the academic domain. To do so, we have provided an overview of two leading theories in motivation: Self-Determination theory (SDT) and Achievement Goal theory (AGT). These two theories are the main theoretical frameworks for the majority of research on perfectionism and academic achievement motivation (Fletcher & Speirs Neumeister, 2012; Stoeber, Damian, & Madigan, 2017).

Self-Determination Theory and Perfectionism

Researchers adopting the SDT framework have examined goal-directed behaviors within the lens of satisfying the innate basic psychological needs of autonomy, competence, and relatedness as motives. In contrast to Behaviorism theories focused on external consequences as motivating behavior, SDT views the possibility that, at times, individuals engage in goal-directed behaviors without consideration of external consequences (Deci & Ryan, 2000). Yet consideration of consequences to motivate behaviors are presumed to exist on a continuum: on one end of the continuum, individuals who engage with tasks without considering the external consequences are viewed as having intrinsic motivation and on the other end of the continuum, individuals who have no motivation to move toward goals are viewed as having amotivation (Deci & Ryan, 2000; Ryan & Deci, 2002). Within the middle of the continuum is extrinsic motivation involving four different forms moving from intrinsic motivation to amotivation: integrated, identified, introjected, and external. The four types of motivation differ in the extent to which individuals have internalized the values and expectations of others and society and incorporated them into their sense of self (Deci & Ryan, 2000; Ryan & Deci, 2002). On one end of this continuum, self-determined, or autonomous, motivations are present when individuals engage in tasks out of curiosity and enjoyment (i.e., intrinsic motivation) or the value attached to the task has been fully integrated into their sense of self (i.e., integrated motivation) or important behaviors have been fully endorsed as valuable (i.e., identified regulation). In each case, individuals are regulating their own behavior in an autonomous manner based on their own internal needs and values. In contrast, controlled motivations are present when individuals have not fully accepted the value of the task. For example, students may engage in tasks because they have internalized the external forces that were previously motivating their behavior such as disappointment from parents, teasing from peers and self-criticism (i.e., introjected regulation). Thus, internal memories or schemes about consequences are still controlling their behavior. For externally motivated students, internal schemes about consequences are not considered, but rather the focus is entirely on the external consequences such as obtaining a good grade or avoiding a low grade (i.e., external regulation). Thus, external and introjected motives of behavior are non-self-determined, or controlled regulations. At the end of the continuum, amotivation would signal no regulation and passive compliance or non-compliance with a task.

Given that perfectionism may be more likely to develop in personally relevant and meaningful achievement situations, researchers have hypothesized that perfectionism, particularly perfectionistic strivings, might be related to intrinsic motivation or autonomous motivation. In contrast, researchers have hypothesized that perfectionistic concerns, with an emphasis on fears of disappointing others and contingent self-worth, are related to controlled motivations. To examine autonomous (i.e., intrinsic) and controlled (i.e., extrinsic) motivation and perfectionism, researchers have examined the four different types of motivation: intrinsic, identified, introjected, external (Stoeber, Feast, & Hayward, 2009) or used these subscales to create an index of self-determined motivation (Gaudreau & Thompson, 2010; Gaudreau, Franche, & Gareau, 2016; Mills & Blankstein, 2000; Miquelon, Vallerand, Grouzet, & Cardinal, 2005). Using the Hewitt and Flett (1991) Multidimensional Perfectionism Scale (HFMPS), self-oriented perfectionism was related to intrinsic motivation whereas socially prescribed perfectionism was related to extrinsic motivation (Miquelon et al., 2005; Stoeber et al., 2009). Socially prescribed perfectionism was also found to have a negative relationship with intrinsic motivation (Mills & Blankstein, 2000; Stoeber et al., 2009). Perfectionistic strivings, as measured by the short version (Cox, Enns, & Clara, 2002) of the HFMPS and Frost Multidimensional Perfectionism Scale (FMPS; Frost, Marten, Lahart, & Rosenblate, 1990), were associated with higher levels of intrinsic motivation than mixed perfectionism (i.e., high levels of perfectionistic strivings and perfectionistic concerns) and non-perfectionism (Gaudreau & Thompson, 2010; Gaudreau et al., 2016). Perfectionistic concerns were associated with lower levels of intrinsic motivation than non-perfectionism and mixed perfectionism (Gaudreau & Thompson, 2010; Gaudreau et al., 2016). Inconsistent with other research, Mills and Blankstein (2000) found that self-oriented perfectionism and socially prescribed perfectionism were correlated with extrinsic motivation, perhaps due to their use of a different measure for motivation—the Work Preference Inventory (Amabile, Hill, Hennessey, & Tighe, 1994). Consistent across the majority of studies, perfectionistic strivings were related to intrinsic motivation whereas perfectionistic concerns were related to extrinsic motivation.

Different motivation profiles for students with perfectionism might explain important outcomes related to the general trend of perfectionistic strivings related to higher academic achievement and perfectionistic concerns related to lower academic achievement (see Chapter 1). Controlling for the four different types of motivation, socially prescribed perfectionism still predicted total test anxiety scores, but not self-oriented perfectionism (Stoeber et al., 2009). Thus, perfectionistic concerns explained test anxiety despite accounting for higher levels of extrinsic motivation. Using the Academic Motivation Scale (Vallerand et al., 1993) to create a self-determined motivation index ranging from non-self-determined to self-determined motivation, Miquelon et al. (2005) examined perfectionism (beginning of the semester—Time 1), self-determined motivation (middle of the semester—Time 2), and psychological adjustment, as measured by the General Health Questionnaire (Goldberg & Hillier, 1979) using the subscales for anxiety and social dysfunction (Time 1 and end of the semester—Time 3). Self-determined academic motivation mediated the relationship between self-oriented perfectionism and fewer psychological adjustment problems, whereas non-self-determined perfectionism mediated the relationship between socially prescribed perfectionism and higher adjustment problems. In Study 2, self-determined motivation mediated the positive relationship between self-oriented perfectionism and academic adjustment (Miquelon et al., 2005). Non-self-determined motivation was not related to academic adjustment, thus mediation was not examined. Using structural equation modeling to examine the 2 × 2 model of dispositional perfectionism, Gaudreau et al. (2016) reported that academic self-determined motivation mediated the relationship between perfectionism subtypes and academic satisfaction. These findings suggest that students with perfectionistic strivings have more readily internalized the value and importance of academic work, leading to lower anxiety, higher academic satisfaction, and higher academic adjustment. In contrast, higher anxiety, lower academic satisfaction, and lower academic adjustment are likely characteristics of students with perfectionistic concerns and low levels of self-determined motivation. When the 2 × 2 dispositional model of perfectionism was examined, mixed perfectionism seems to be associated with partially internalized reasons for pursuing academic achievements (i.e., introjected regulation), which may help off-set the detrimental effects of perfectionistic concerns (Gaudreau et al., 2016).

Future Research on SDT and Perfectionism in the Academic Context

Although intrinsic and extrinsic motivation may serve as mediators between perfectionism and direct measures of academic achievement such as GPA or course grades, there has been no research that has exam-ined self-determined motivation as a mediator for this relationship. Yet research with other measures such as academic adjustment (Miquelon et al., 2005) and academic satisfaction (Gaudreau et al., 2016) suggest that intrinsic and extrinsic motivation may be important mediators between perfectionism and academic achievement. In the domain of work, Stoeber and Damian (2016) have proposed a theoretical model in which autonomous motivations mediate the inverse relationship between perfectionistic strivings and work burnout and controlled motivations mediate the positive relationship between perfectionistic concerns and work burnout. As students' academic burnout is also a concern for edu-cators, systematic investigations of perfectionism and motivation are crucial. Future research should examine such questions, given the impor-tance of students' motivation in school reform (Usher & Kober, 2012; National Research Council, 2004).

Achievement Goal Theory and Perfectionism

Another theoretical approach that has been adopted to investigate per-fectionism and achievement motivation is AGT. Elliot and his colleagues (Elliot, 1997, Elliot & Church, 1997) have developed a theoretical model based on combining achievement motives—need for achievement and fear of failure—with achievement goals. Achievement goal researchers have sought to understand why students strive for achievement: to master certain knowledge or skills (mastery) or to perform relative to others (performance). Central to the discussion of achievement motivation is goal orientation. Elliot (1997) defined a 2 × 2 goal orientation framework based on the definition of competence and the valence. Competence, defined by the standard on which it is evaluated, can be absolute and intrapersonal (mastery) or based on normative comparison (performance). Competence may be valenced in terms of whether it centers on the positive possibility of displaying one's competence (approach) or the negative possibility of displaying one's incompetence (avoidance) (Elliot, 1997).

When these two dimensions are crossed, four distinct achievement goals emerge: mastery approach, mastery avoidance, performance approach, and performance avoidance (Elliot, 1997; Elliot & Church, 1997). Mastery approach goals are indicative when individuals strive to achieve intrapersonal, absolute competence (e.g., running a marathon in a certain time). Mastery avoidance goals are indicative when individuals strive to avoid intrapersonal incompetence (e.g., striving not to record a longer time while running the next marathon). Performance approach goals are indicative when individuals set a goal to achieve competence relative to other people (e.g., to finish before a friend in the marathon). Finally, performance avoidance goals are indicative when individuals set goals to avoid appearing incompetent relative to others (e.g., goal to not quit the race if friends do not quit). Achievement goal orientation theory with this 2 × 2 framework has stimulated a wealth of research on perfectionism and achievement motivation.

AGT has been a popular theoretical framework for the study of motivation and perfectionism because of the overlapping constructs of need for achievement (approach—perfectionistic strivings) and fear of failure (avoidance—perfectionistic concerns). Moreover, concerns about appearing perfect to others and gaining the approval of others intersect with performance goals. Researchers have mostly focused on three different types of achievement goals—mastery approach, performance approach, and performance avoidance—to examine relationships with perfectionism (Bong, Hwang, Noh, & Kim, 2014; Damian, Stoeber, Negru, & Baban, 2014; Eum & Rice, 2011; Fletcher, Shim, & Wang, 2012; Hanchon, 2010; Speirs Neumeister, Fletcher, & Burney, 2015; Speirs Neumeister &

Finch, 2006; Vansteenkiste et al., 2010; Van Yperen, 2006; Verner-Filion & Gaudreau, 2010). Only three studies were found that also included mastery avoidance goals (Damian et al., 2014; Eum & Rice, 2011; Van Yperen, 2006), although this type of goal might be particularly relevant to perfectionists (Elliot, 2005). Most of these studies have employed the HFMPS or the FMPS measures of perfectionism and versions of the Achievement Goal Questionnaire (AGQ; Elliot & McGregor, 2001) to examine mastery approach, performance approach, and performance avoidance.

Regardless of the perfectionism measure, perfectionistic concerns related to performance approach and/or performance avoidance goals across all relevant studies (Bong et al., 2014; Damian et al., 2014; Eum & Rice, 2011; Fletcher et al., 2012; Hanchon, 2010; Speirs Neumeister et al., 2015; Speirs Neumeister & Finch, 2006; Vansteenkiste et al., 2010; Van Yperen, 2006; Verner-Filion & Gaudreau, 2010). Students with perfectionistic concerns appear to be focused on what others expect of them and how others evaluate them. Thus, students with perfectionistic concerns will be more likely to adopt performance goals that are based on outperforming others (Damian et al., 2014) and less likely to adopt mastery goals focused on mastery and learning for oneself (Verner-Filion & Gaudreau, 2010).

Mastery goal orientations involve a focus on the self and personal standards: the core of perfectionistic strivings (Damian et al., 2014). Consistent with this, perfectionistic strivings have been linked to mastery approach goals as well as performance approach and performance avoidance goals. Using the Almost Perfect Scale-Revised (APS-R; Slaney & Johnson, 2001), Eum and Rice (2011) found that high standards were related to mastery approach and performance approach goals. Mastery approach, performance approach, and performance avoidance goals were related to self-oriented perfectionism in several studies (Speirs Neumeister & Finch, 2006; Van Yperen, 2006; Verner-Filion & Gaudreau, 2010). Perfectionistic strivings, as measured by personal standards from the FMPS, were related to mastery approach, performance approach, and performance avoidance goals, whereas organization was only related to mastery approach and performance approach goals (Fletcher et al., 2012). When controlling for socially prescribed perfectionism in regression analyses,

Damian and colleagues (2014) reported that self-oriented perfectionism positively predicted mastery approach and mastery avoidance goals. Similarly, within a structural equation model, Bong et al. (2014) reported a significant relationship between self-oriented perfectionism and mastery approach goals (i.e., mastery avoidance was not included in the model).

Using Gaudreau and Thompson's (2010) 2 × 2 model of dispositional perfectionism, Speirs Neumeister, Fletcher, and Burney (2015) investigated the relationship between perfectionism and achievement goal orientation. In a sample of honors college students, perfectionistic strivings (i.e., self-oriented perfectionism) related to higher levels of mastery approach and performance approach goals compared with non-perfectionism. Mixed perfectionism (i.e., high self-oriented and high socially prescribed) related to higher levels of mastery approach and performance approach goals compared with perfectionistic concerns (i.e., socially prescribed). Perfectionistic strivings related to higher levels of mastery approach goals than perfectionistic concerns (Cohen's d = 0.71) but not performance approach goals (Cohen's d = 0.32). However, *this same pattern was reported for performance avoidance goals*, deviating from the hypothesized relationships of Gaudreau (2012) for negative outcomes: perfectionistic strivings were related to higher levels of performance avoidance goals compared with non-perfectionism. Mixed perfectionism related to higher levels of performance avoidance goals compared with perfectionistic concerns. Finally, perfectionistic strivings and perfectionistic concerns did not differ for performance avoidance goals.

In summary, perfectionistic concerns have been associated with performance approach and performance avoidance goals. Students with perfectionistic concerns are anxious about how others view them and fear potential criticism from others. Yet students with perfectionistic strivings seem to have the same concerns. In fact, mixed perfectionism was related to significantly higher levels of performance avoidance goals than perfectionistic concerns (Speirs Neumeister et al., 2015). This general trend supports the hypothesis of Flett and Hewitt (2006) that individuals with perfectionism, regardless of the type of perfectionism, experience an approach/avoidance motivational conflict in their academic work. In other words, students with perfectionism set exceedingly high personal standards and approach academic assignments to gain mastery and demonstrate competence, yet are also plagued by worry that they will be viewed as incompetent upon evaluation. This motivational conflict has been referred to as a double-edged sword (Fletcher et al., 2012; Stoeber, 2014): contrasting behaviors related to goals for achievement (approach) and goals for avoiding failure (avoidance).

Differences in achievement goal orientations for students with perfectionistic strivings and students with perfectionistic concerns suggest a strong theoretical basis for achievement goals as potential mediators for the relationship between perfectionism and academic achievement. However, research findings have been inconclusive. For example, in a study of seventh grade Korean students, Bong et al. (2014) examined academic self-efficacy (i.e., one's confidence in the ability to perform a certain academic task to the desired level) and achievement goal orientation as potential mediators for the relationship between perfectionism and academic achievement in English and math, as measured by final exam scores. Only self-oriented perfectionism, not socially prescribed perfectionism, was related to academic achievement in English and math. However, this relationship was not mediated by performance approach goals as hypothesized (Bong et al., 2014).

Vernon-Filion and Gaudreau (2010) also conducted a mediation study of perfectionism, achievement goals, and academic achievement. In this study, self-oriented perfectionism predicted GPA and was positively related to mastery approach, performance approach, and performance avoidance goals. Socially prescribed perfectionism negatively predicted GPA and was negatively related to mastery approach goals and positively related to performance approach and performance avoidance goals. However, the paths between perfectionism and GPAs were mediated by goal orientation: the positive relationship between self-oriented perfectionism and GPA was partially mediated by performance approach goals. Moreover, the negative relationship between socially prescribed perfectionism and GPA was also partially mediated by performance approach goals. Mediation studies such as these two studies illustrate the complex routes to explain how different types of perfectionism connect to achievement. Much more research is necessary to understand how motivation may mediate the relationship between perfectionism and academic achievement. To date, mediation studies for motivation and perfectionism have used the HFMPS and the AGT framework. More research is needed to examine achievement goals as mediators using different measures, or combined measures, of perfectionism.

Future Research on AGT and Perfectionism in the Academic Context

Elliot, Murayama, and Pekrun (2011) recently updated their theoretical framework with a 3×2 version of this model. The new addition differentiates between absolute (mastery of the task) and intrapersonal (doing better than one's past performance) as standards of comparison. As such, the new model includes three dimensions yielding six different achievement goals: task-approach is trying to master a task (e.g., to learn the information in a class), task-avoidance is avoiding not being able to master the task (e.g., avoid answering incorrectly in class), self-approach is to do better than one has done in the past (e.g., get a higher score than before on a math quiz), self-avoidance is avoiding doing worse than one has done before (e.g., not getting a lower score than previous score on a math quiz), other-approach is striving to do better than others (e.g., earning the highest score on the math quiz), and other-avoidance is to avoid doing worse than others (e.g., not performing worse than others on the math quiz). Only one study was found that used the six achievement goals from the 3×2 model to examine exam performance (Stoeber, Haskew, & Scott, 2015). Using the 3×2 AGQ (Elliot et al., 2011), students were asked to complete the HFMPS (Time 1) and were given a chapter to study for an upcoming exam. Students then made an appointment to take the exam on the chapter and complete the AGQ (Time 2). Self-oriented perfectionism was positively correlated with exam performance and each of the six achievement goals, whereas socially prescribed perfectionism was only positively correlated with other-approach goals. In regression analyses, task-approach goals were the only achievement goal that predicted exam performance. Moreover, the relationship between exam performance and self-oriented perfectionism was mediated by task-approach goals (Stoeber et al., 2015). Results from this study suggest a major departure from the research findings on achievement goals and perfectionism using the 2 × 2 AGT theoretical model. Much more research is needed in this area.

Parenting and Achievement Motivation

Within the wealth of research on parenting and perfectionism (see Chapter 3), a few studies have examined how different types of parenting might influence achievement motivation for students with perfectionism. According to SDT, the need for autonomy drives motivation and certain types of parenting, such as authoritarian and psychologically controlling parenting, diminish children's autonomy. Authoritarian and controlling parenting leads to children's adoption of extrinsic motivations and performance goals, and this relationship may be influenced by children's perfectionistic concerns. When adolescent athletes perceived that they had family climates with rigid control and rules, athletes reported higher levels of extrinsic motivation compared to athletes who perceived that they had an egalitarian family climate (McArdle & Duda, 2004). With regard to psychologically controlling parenting, Fletcher et al. (2012) reported that psychologically controlling parenting was significantly related to performance approach and performance avoidance goals; however, concern over mistakes fully mediated this relationship. Parenting practices that involve control contribute to the development of students' perfectionistic concerns that, in turn, may lead to adopting an achievement motivation profile focused on competition, comparison to others and external rewards.

According to Flett and colleagues (2002), the extent to which children internalize parents' expectations and goals may be an important mediator for perfectionistic traits. Tong and Lam (2011) examined Chinese mothers and their 7- to 9-year-old children on measures of children's perfectionism, mothers' performance goals for their child, and children's willing to internalize their mothers' values. Children's self-oriented perfectionism moderated the relationship between mothers' performance goals for their child and children's willingness to internalize those goals. When children were more willing to internalize their mother's values, children's self-oriented perfectionism was associated with their mothers' high performance goals. Children's socially prescribed perfectionism was not related to mothers' performance goals for them. Although much more research is needed, children's willingness to internalize parental goals and expectations may be an important factor to understanding the connection between perfectionism and motivation.

Summary

Together, the results of the studies on perfectionism and achievement motivations in the academic domain have yielded quite consistent findings (Stoeber et al., 2017). Perfectionistic concerns are associated with controlled motivations and performance approach and performance avoidance goals. Students with perfectionistic concerns are driven to achieve academically to meet the expectations of perfection from others and avoid self-criticism and self-blame. Part of pleasing other people such as teachers and parents and avoiding self-deprecation may involve demonstrating superior competence over others plus trying to hide incompetence. Yet this is not unique to students with perfectionistic concerns. Students with perfectionistic strivings are also preoccupied with how their academic performance compares to others.

However, for students with perfectionistic strivings, a mixed profile of controlled and autonomous and mastery and performance goals might not hurt academic achievement. Using a group approach, profiles for students with high autonomous and high controlled motivations resulted in the highest academic adjustment in adolescents (Ratelle, Guay, Vallerand, Larose, & Senecal, 2007). High mastery approach goals and high performance approach goals are associated with higher academic performance (Harackiewicz, Barron, Carter, Lehto, & Elliot, 1997; Harackiewicz, Barron, & Elliot, 1998). Academic motivation and achievement are most likely to suffer when students endorse performance avoidance goals such as students with perfectionistic concerns do (Church, Elliot, & Gable, 2001; Elliot & McGregor, 1999; Elliot, 2005). But mastery goals and autonomous motivations, adopted by students with high perfectionistic strivings, may buffer them from the negative effects of performance avoidance goals, allowing them to reach important goals (Stoeber et al., 2017). Mastery goals seemed to protect gifted students with perfectionistic concerns (but low contingent self-worth) from having low levels of academic self-efficacy (Wang, Fu, & Rice, 2012).

Future research will be necessary to untangle how mixed profiles of achievement goals and autonomous/controlled motivations adopted by students with perfectionism impact academic achievement. Researchers have demonstrated that students with high intrinsic aspirations endorsed mastery approach goals more, performance approach goals less, and had higher grades than students with lower levels of intrinsic aspirations (Mouratidis, Vansteenkiste, Lens, Michou, & Soenens, 2013). Vansteenkiste et al. (2010) reported that perfectionistic strivings were related to autonomous reasons for performance approach goals, whereas perfectionistic concerns were related to controlled reasons for performance approach goals. Future studies that include achievement goals and autonomous/controlled motivations may provide a more nuanced picture of the relationship between perfectionism and achievement motivation. Researchers also need to consider contextually dependent variables such as domain-specific task value in different academic subject areas. To date, researchers have only considered academics in general, examining self-reported achievement motivations across all academic subjects. When researchers have focused on specific coursework, they have selected English and/or math (Bong et al., 2014; Shim, Rubenstein, & Drapeau, 2016): required subject areas as opposed to selected courses and electives. Similar to the sports domain, students may have heightened intrinsic interest for specific academic goals, such as courses for their college major or high school courses that they have selected. Perfectionistic traits may only be expressed in this subject area but not other subjects. The use of daily diary methods, similar to the work of Dunkley and colleagues (Dunkley, Zuroff, & Blankstein, 2003), might hold promise. For example, Harvey et al. (2015) recruited undergraduates to complete measures of self-critical perfectionism (DEQ; Blatt, D'Afflitti, & Quinlan, 1976) and self-oriented perfectionism as well as listing four academic goals, goal motivations (autonomous vs. controlled), and goal progress. Self-critical perfectionism was related to fewer academic goals and controlled motivation toward those goals, whereas self-oriented perfectionism was related to more academic goals and autonomous motivation toward those goals (Harvey et al., 2015). In this study, students were able to report goals that were meaningful to them and describe their reasons for pursuing those goals as opposed to general survey questions. Researchers will need to find ways such as diary methods and/or interviews to determine how individuals may develop intense interests about specific content areas and how those interests may influence the expression of perfectionistic traits.

CHAPTER 5

Responses to Academic Expectations and Perfectionism

Students with perfectionism who are dealing with the demands of harsh and controlling parents and compromised motivation toward their academic work are likely under considerable stress. Although moderate amounts of stress help to urge students to prepare and study for academic work, high levels of stress may produce dysfunctional academic outcomes such as burnout, test anxiety, and procrastination. Less well documented, however, is how high levels of academic stress interact with students' perfectionism. In their meta-analysis on perfectionism and burnout across work, sports, and academics domains, Hill and Curran (2016) revealed that perfectionistic strivings had a negative relationship with burnout whereas perfectionistic concerns had a positive relationship with burnout. Students with perfectionistic concerns also seem to have higher levels of test anxiety and academic procrastination. In contrast, students with perfectionistic strivings reported lower levels of test anxiety and academic procrastination together with higher levels of engagement with their academic work. The purpose of this chapter is to review the literature on perfectionism and these academic behaviors to determine their influence on academic achievement.

Academic Stress and Burnout

Recent studies have specifically examined the relationship between perfectionism and stress in undergraduate students who are likely to experience academic stress. Examining undergraduate honors students, Rice, Leever, Christopher, and Porter (2006) measured perfectionism, perceived stress, and academic adjustment at the beginning and end of a semester. Students were also asked about their satisfaction with their academic experiences and performance. At the beginning of the semester, the subscale of discrepancy interacted with perceived stress but the subscale of high standards did not. When students' perceived stress was high and discrepancy was high, satisfaction with their academic experiences and performance was significantly lower than when discrepancy was high and perceived stress was low. Moreover, perceived stress mediated the relationship between discrepancy and academic satisfaction. During times of increased stress (midterm and finals week), individuals with high discrepancy experienced more anxiety surrounding their academic performance.

In another study of stress, three groups of science, technology, engineering, or mathematics (STEM) majors (perfectionistic strivings perfectionists, perfectionistic concerns perfectionists, and non-perfectionists) reported on their academic and personal stress over an academic year (Rice, Richardson, & Ray, 2016). Over the course of the year, undergraduate STEM majors in the perfectionistic concerns group transitioned into patterns of moderate or high stress, but none of the perfectionistic concerns perfectionists transitioned into a pattern of low stress. In contrast, equal distributions of the perfectionistic strivings group transitioned into low and moderate stress patterns. Interestingly, females with perfectionistic concerns were more likely to transition into high stress patterns over the academic year compared to males with perfectionistic concerns. These stress patterns did impact GPA (i.e., grade point average): those perfectionistic concerns perfectionists moving into reported high stress had lower GPAs in their STEM courses compared to perfectionistic strivings perfectionists who reported low stress across the year. Although Rice and colleagues (2006, 2016) demonstrated that perfectionistic concerns, particularly in females, lead to increased perceived stress, the measure of perceived stress was based on combining responses to questions about stress for academic and personal problems. Thus, the combination of academic and personal stress into one perceived stress measure makes it difficult to pinpoint the specific effects of academic stress on GPA.

Interactions between increasing academic stress over time for perfectionistic concerns perfectionists likely place them at risk for reduced achievement and academic burnout. Academic burnout involves exhaustion from studying, cynical attitudes toward academic work, and low academic self-efficacy and feelings of incompetence (see Walburg, 2014 for a review). Various levels of exhaustion, cynicism, and academic efficacy were found for individual students, creating different profiles of students with academic burnout (Lee et al., 2010; Shih, 2015). Exhaustion, cynicism, and feeling of incompetence have been shown to increase from 4th to 12th grades in cross-sectional research (Lee, Puig, Lea, & Lee, 2013). Longitudinal research, however, revealed that higher initial levels of emotional exhaustion were associated with higher increases in cynicism and academic inefficacy in South Korean middle school students (Kim, Lee, Kim, Choi, & Lee, 2015). As such, emotional exhaustion in students may be the first sign of academic burnout, supporting the idea of a continuum from academic stress to academic burnout (Salmela-Aro, Kiuru, & Nurmi, 2008).

Understanding the development of academic burnout is critical, given the negative consequences for students' academic achievement. Examining undergraduate students in Spain, Portugal, and the Netherlands, Schaufeli, Martinez, Marques Pinto, Salanova, and Bakker (2002) found that emotional exhaustion, cynicism, and reduced academic efficacy were negatively correlated with academic success, as measured by the proportion of exams passed during the previous academic term. Reduced academic achievement and school engagement have also been associated with academic stress and burnout in adolescent samples (Tuominen-Soini & Salmela-Aro, 2013) and reduced GPA and cognitive functioning in college samples (May, Bauer, & Fincham, 2015). In addition to academic achievement, academic burnout has been associated with adolescents increased risk for poor mental health outcomes (Walburg, 2014).

Academic burnout and its consequences might be particularly problematic for students with perfectionistic concerns due to additional stress caused by harsh and rigid self-evaluations of one's performance added to perceptions of exceedingly high expectations from others (Hill & Curran, 2016). Consequently, students who are preoccupied with living up to standards of others and are in constant need for self-validation from others likely suffer from academic burnout. Studies on academic burnout and perfectionism have reported that perfectionistic strivings were either not correlated or negatively correlated with academic burnout and perfectionistic concerns were positively correlated with academic burnout in adolescents and undergraduates (Chang, Lee, Byeon, & Lee, 2015; Chang, Lee, Byeon, Seong, & Lee, 2016; Shih, 2012). Using the Frost Multidimensional Perfectionism Scale (FMPS; Frost, Marten, Lahart, & Rosenblate, 1990) with eighth grade Taiwanese students, personal standards and organization had an inverse relationship with exhaustion, cynicism, and inefficacy, whereas concern over mistakes and doubts about actions positively predicted all three burnout dimensions (Shih, 2012). The same pattern was found in Korean high school students (Chang et al., 2015) and Korean undergraduates (Chang et al., 2016) using the Hewitt and Flett Multidimensional Perfectionism Scale (HFMPS; Hewitt & Flett, 1991).

However, motivation may influence the relationship between perfectionism and academic burnout. Shih (2012) found that once mastery and performance achievement goals were entered into the regression model, perfectionistic strivings were no longer significantly related to the burnout dimensions, while perfectionism concerns still predicted the burnout dimensions. In two separate studies, one with Korean high school students (Chang et al., 2015) and one with undergraduates (Chang et al., 2016), intrinsic motivation partially mediated the negative relationship between self-oriented perfectionism and academic burnout. In contrast, extrinsic motivation fully mediated the positive relationship between socially prescribed perfectionism and academic burnout.

Academic burnout is the opposite of academic engagement, with measures of engagement and burnout having negative correlations in a large multinational study (Schaufeli et al., 2002). Academic engagement has also been conceptualized as a multidimensional construct, including dimensions associated with vigor (i.e., energy and willingness to engage with work), dedication, and absorption. Researchers have hypothesized that academic engagement would be positively related to perfectionistic strivings and negatively related to perfectionistic concerns. In support of these hypotheses, concern over mistakes and doubts about actions were negatively related to vigor and dedication dimensions; in addition, personal standards and organization were positively related to all three dimensions of engagement in eighth grade Taiwanese students (Shih, 2012). Using the FMPS with Chinese undergraduate students, Zhang , Gan, and Cham (2007) also found that personal standards and organization predicted academic engagement. In a longitudinal study, Damian, Stoeber, Negru-Subtirica, and Baban (2017) examined school engagement in 6th to 12th graders at three time points (every four to five months) using the School Engagement Measure-MacArthur (SEM-MacArther; Fredricks, Blumenfeld, Friedel, & Paris, 2005) to capture behavioral, emotional, and cognitive engagement. Combining subscales from the Child-Adolescent Perfectionism Scale (CAPS; Flett et al., 2016) and FMPS, they found that perfectionistic strivings, but not perfectionistic concerns, predicted increased cognitive engagement in school over time but not behavioral or emotional engagement in school (Damian et al., 2017). In contrast, behavioral engagement and emotional engagement in math were positively related to personal standards in middle school students (Shim, Rubenstein, & Drapeau, 2016).

Future Research on Stress and Burnout and Perfectionism in the Academic Context

One important area of future research will be to investigate possible continuum from academic stress to academic burnout (Salmela-Aro et al., 2008). What are the signals when students with perfectionistic concerns are experiencing the extreme stress and exhaustion leading to academic burnout? Answers to this research question may provide methods to assess students with perfectionistic concerns that are at risk for academic burnout and target them for intervention. Each of the studies on academic burnout used a dimensional data analysis approach with no studies using a group approach. What about students who have high levels of perfectionistic strivings and high levels of perfectionistic concerns? Cluster analysis or cut-off scores, using the Almost Perfect Scale-Revised (Slaney, Rice, Mobley, Trippi, & Ashby, 2001) may be used to examine different groups of students with perfectionism and academic burnout.

Test Anxiety

Despite recent research on emotional engagement and perfectionism (Damian et al., 2017; Shim et al., 2016), there has been limited research conducted on perfectionism and academic emotions. Academic emotions refer to emotional experiences that occur in academic settings and/or are connected to academic work (Pekrun & Stephens, 2012). Emotions related to academic work within or outside of school encompass a range of positive (e.g., joy, hope, pride) and negative emotions (e.g., anger, anxiety, sadness). In addition to conceptualizing positive and negative academic emotions, Pekrun and colleagues (Pekrun, 2006; Pekrun, Goetz, Titz, & Perry, 2002) have differentiated between activity emotions and outcome emotions. Activity emotions refer to students' emotional experiences as they are engaged with academic activities such as studying or in class. Outcome emotions refer to emotions about success and failure on upcoming academic evaluations and emotions about past success and failure.

Students' outcome emotions have received the bulk of research attention, mainly in the area of test anxiety (Cassady, 2010; Hembree, 1988; Zeidner, 1998; Zeidner & Matthews, 2005). Test anxiety involves heightened cognitions and emotions associated with evaluative situations and include multiple dimensions such as worry, emotionality (i.e., physiological reactions to evaluations), interference, and lack of confidence (Liebert & Morris, 1967; Zeidner, 1998). In addition to experiencing emotions during evaluations, Cassady (2004; 2010) has argued that test anxiety also impacts the three stages of the learning–testing cycle: test preparation, test performance, and test reflection. As such, students may suffer the effects of test anxiety at any one stage and/or any combination of stages in this cycle. Understanding the consequences of test anxiety for students is critical, given reported negative correlations between test anxiety and cognitive performance (Hembree, 1988; Seipp, 1991) and GPA (Cassady & Johnson, 2002; Chapell et al., 2005). At its core, students' test anxiety involves concern over being evaluated and cognitions about potential failure before, during, and after an evaluation. Because students with perfectionistic concerns are preoccupied with potential mistakes and failure that may disappoint others, students with perfectionistic concerns are at high risk of suffering from test anxiety (Cassady, 2010).

Research has supported the positive connection between perfectionistic concerns and test anxiety across numerous studies (Abdollahi & Talib, 2015; Arana & Furlan, 2016; Bieling, Israeli, & Antony, 2004; Eum & Rice, 2011; Mills & Blankstein, 2000; Stoeber, Feast & Hayward, 2009;

Weiner & Carton, 2012). Significant test anxiety—perfectionistic concerns correlations were reported across studies using different perfectionism measures: HFMPS (Mills & Blankstein, 2000; Stoeber et al., 2009), FMPS (Weiner & Carton, 2012), APS-R (Abdollahi & Talib, 2015; Arana & Furlan, 2016; Eum & Rice, 2011), and combined HFMPS and FMPS (Bieling et al., 2004). In two studies, perfectionistic concerns predicted test anxiety even after controlling for achievement motivation (Eum & Rice, 2011; Stoeber et al., 2009). Specifically, after controlling for intrinsic and extrinsic motivation, perfectionistic concerns predicted interference and lack of confidence but not worry and emotionality (Stoeber et al., 2009). The relationship between perfectionistic concerns and test anxiety was mediated by performance avoidance goals in a sample of Korean middle school students (Bong, Hwang, Noh, & Kim, 2014). In a sample of Iranian high school students, emotional intelligence moderated perfectionism and test anxiety: the negative relationship between discrepancy and test anxiety was significant only for the low emotional intelligence group (Abdollahi & Talib, 2015). That is, students with perfectionistic concerns and high levels of emotional intelligence (i.e., ability to perceive, understand, and manage the emotions of oneself and others) may be less likely to suffer from test anxiety. Results from this research indicate that other factors such as achievement motivation and emotional intelligence may play a role in the relationship between perfectionistic concerns and test anxiety.

Students with perfectionistic concerns may be so overwhelmed with their concerns over disappointing others that they may avoid preparing for tests. Consistent with this hypothesis, Weiner and Carton (2012) found that avoidance coping (e.g., mental and behavioral disengagement from the stressful situation) partially mediated with relationship between test anxiety and perfectionistic concerns, as measured by concern over mistakes and doubts about actions. Examining a specific measure for coping with an upcoming exam, groups with high standards (perfectionistic strivings perfectionists and mixed perfectionists) were more likely to adopt positive coping strategies such as studying compared the perfectionistic concerns and nonperfectionists groups (Arana & Furlan, 2016). So even before testing, students with perfectionistic concerns may avoid and procrastinate studying. When they do study, their study efforts may be less effective because they are preoccupied with a less-than-perfect performance and fear of failure.

The relationship between perfectionistic strivings and test anxiety is less straightforward. Mills and Blankstein (2000) reported positive correlations between self-oriented perfectionism and test anxiety; however, this relationship disappeared after controlling for socially prescribed perfectionism. It should be noted that Mills and Blankstein (2000) did not use a specific measure of test anxiety, but rather examined the subscale for test anxiety from the Motivated Strategies for Learning Questionnaire (MSLQ; Pintrich, Smith, Garcia, & McKeachie, 1993). Also using items from the MSLQ test anxiety subscale, Bong et al. (2014) reported no relationship between self-oriented perfectionism and test anxiety. Using the Test Anxiety Scale (Sarason, 1984), Weiner and Carton (2012) reported a significant negative correlation between personal standards and test anxiety, whereas other studies found no correlation (Bieling et al., 2004; Eum & Rice, 2011). Perfectionistic strivings may have a more nuanced relationship with test anxiety. When Stoeber and colleagues (2009) used a multidimensional measure of test anxiety (Test Anxiety Inventory; Hodapp, Glanzmann, & Laux, 1995), self-oriented perfectionism had a positive correlation with worry and negative correlations with interference and lack of confidence, after controlling for socially prescribed perfectionism. Using the APS-R, Arana and Furlan (2016) also reported that high standards were correlated with worry as well as emotionality. Moreover, using a group-based approach, the perfectionistic strivings group and the perfectionistic concerns group had similar levels of worry (Arana & Furlan, 2016). Thus students with perfectionistic strivings may worry about the potential outcomes of evaluative situations, yet are able to focus on the task and feel confident in their ability to prepare for evaluations and meet their high achievement standards (Stoeber et al., 2009).

Future Research on Test Anxiety and Perfectionism in the Academic Context

Although much more work is needed, students with perfectionistic concerns may suffer from cognitions surrounding failure and disappointing others at each phase of the learning–testing cycle (Cassady, 2010).

Preliminary evidence supports that disappointing highly demanding parents contributes to test anxiety for students with perfectionistic concerns (Soysa & Weiss, 2014). Before an exam, last minute studying or ineffective preparation will decrease students with perfectionistic concerns' self-confidence even before they see the exam questions (Arana & Furlan, 2016; Weiner & Carton, 2012). During the actual test, students with perfectionistic concerns will find it much more difficult to focus on test questions due to intruding thoughts of potential failure. Worry and rumination about potential mistakes and failure after a test are likely to continue to haunt students with perfectionistic concerns, thereby further reducing their ability to move on to their next academic task. Research related to how perfectionism might impact students before, during, and after an evaluation is needed to target intervention efforts.

Academic Procrastination

Students with perfectionistic strivings may reduce their anxiety surrounding tests and exams by studying well before the test, yet it is unlikely that students with perfectionistic concerns do. Given that students with perfectionistic concerns often use avoidant coping, they probably avoid studying as long as possible. Procrastination is defined as "the act of needlessly delaying tasks to the point of experiencing subjective discomfort" (p. 503; Solomon & Rothblum, 1984). Academic procrastination refers to specific procrastination for academic tasks and students across different countries reported that they frequently procrastinated on academic tasks, with up to 70 percent of students in some studies (Ferrari & Sapadin, 2014). This high percentage of student procrastination is alarming, given that academic procrastination was negatively correlated with academic performance (Kim & Seo, 2015) and procrastination, in general, was positively correlated with avoidant coping (Sirois & Kitner, 2015). Academic procrastination can be viewed as an avoidant coping strategy to delay completing unpleasant or challenging academic tasks (Blunt & Pychyl, 2000).

Early studies of academic procrastination have indicated potential overlap with perfectionism. In one of the first articles related to academic procrastination, Solomon and Rothblum (1984) examined factors that predicted self-reported academic procrastination in college students. Factor analysis on the measure related to reasons for procrastination (PASS: Procrastination Assessment Scale-Students; Solomon & Rothblum, 1984) revealed that factor 1 accounted for 49 percent of the variance and included items related to "anxiety about meeting other's expectations (evaluation anxiety), concern about meeting one's own standards (perfectionism), and lack of self-confidence" (p. 507). Thus perfectionism dimensions were prominent in students' reported reasons for academic procrastination. Studies of academic procrastination and perfectionism using a unidimensional perspective of perfectionism revealed positive associations (Brownlow & Resingler, 2000; Burns, Dittmann, Nguyen, & Mitchelson, 2000). In a chapter titled, *Description and Counseling of the Perfectionistic Procrastinator*, Flett, Hewitt, Davis, and Sherry (2004) revealed that perfectionistic concerns were often positively correlated with procrastination, whereas perfectionistic strivings were not associated with procrastination. Specific to academic procrastination, Flett, Blankstein, Hewitt, and Koledin (1992) reported that socially prescribed perfectionism was correlated with academic procrastination, although self-oriented perfectionism also associated with the fear of failure subscale. Fear of failure, a main construct underlying perfectionistic concerns, has been suggested to play a prominent role in explaining the link between perfectionism and procrastination (Egan, Wade, & Shafran, 2011; Flett et al., 2004).

Research supports the connection between perfectionistic concerns and academic procrastination (for a recent meta-analysis, see Sirois, Molnar, & Hirsch, in press). Burnam, Komarraju, Hamel, and Nadler (2014) asked undergraduate students if procrastination was a problem across various academic tasks such as writing a term paper, studying for exams, and keeping up with weekly reading assignments. Using the FMPS, personal standards had a significant negative association with procrastination problems, whereas concern over mistakes had a significant positive association. This same pattern was found in Korean middle school students for academic procrastination for math (Bong et al., 2014): self-oriented perfectionism was negatively correlated with procrastination and socially prescribed perfectionism was positively correlated with procrastination. Similarly, general procrastination had a significant negative relationship with personal standards and significant positive relationship with doubts about actions in undergraduate students (Ozer, O'Callaghan, Bokszczanin, Ederer, & Essau, 2014). In one of the few longitudinal studies, Rice, Richardson, and Clark (2012) examined perfectionistic concerns and procrastination in undergraduate students at the beginning, middle, and end of the semester. At the beginning of the semester, students with low levels of discrepancy and low levels of procrastination were less likely to experience psychological distress compared to students with low levels of discrepancy and high levels of procrastination. Students with high levels of discrepancy, regardless of their tendency to procrastinate, had similar levels of psychological distress. Perfectionism and procrastination were both very stable across the three time points. Whereas Rice at el. (2012) only examined perfectionistic concerns and academic procrastination, Seo (2008) only examined perfectionism strivings and academic procrastination. Self-oriented perfectionism was negatively correlated with academic procrastination in undergraduates. Moreover, self-efficacy fully mediated the relationship between self-oriented perfectionism and academic procrastination (Seo, 2008).

Future Research on Procrastination and Perfectionism in the Academic Context

Students with perfectionistic concerns likely focus on cognitions about failing and disappointing others even as they contemplate studying or working on academic tasks and thus, likely avoiding them as long as possible. Think about it—if studying for a test makes a student anxious, why would they endure that anxiety for over several hours across several days, say a total of six hours? If their immediate goal is to reduce anxiety, wouldn't it be more adaptive to only study three hours the night before the test? Again, if their goal is to reduce anxiety, and anxiety is present during studying for tests, then students have reduced their time to experience anxiety in half. This example is simplistic but perhaps illustrates a main point: for students with perfectionistic concerns, academic procrastination may reduce the length of time that they have to confront their fears of failure, disappointing others, and facing potential criticism. Additionally, when students are running out of time for a deadline, perfectionistic strivings may "take over" the students' motivational, attention and cognitive resources to focus on the academic task at hand, and in effect, reduce attention to their perfectionistic concerns. However, this is simply speculation. Much more research is needed to determine the interplay between anxiety during academic work and why students with perfectionistic concerns procrastinate their academic work. One clue as to why students with perfectionistic concerns procrastinate might be the fear of harsh criticism from highly demanding parents: academic procrastination and perfectionistic concerns mediated the relationship between authoritarian parents and test anxiety (Soysa & Weiss, 2014).

Summary

Students with perfectionistic concerns are at high risk for academic burnout, test anxiety, and academic procrastination, or even worse, some combination of the three. Separately, and certainly in combination, academic burnout, test anxiety, and academic procrastination will confer risk for decreased academic achievement and increased stress associated with academic work. There is an old saying that "desperate people do desperate things." Students with perfectionistic concerns who are overcome with stress and anxiety may engage in cheating and/or plagiarism. In fact, socially prescribed perfectionism was positively correlated with acceptable attitudes toward cheating in adolescents (Bong et al., 2014), but other studies have not found links between perfectionistic concerns and cheating (Vansteenkiste et al., 2010). When academic stress overwhelms students with perfectionistic concerns, they may have limited coping strategies and resort to dishonest academic practices, or in the case of academic burnout, suffer from a host of negative emotions and attitudes related to their academic work. Students who face academic burnout may be more likely to leave college before graduation, leading to decreased retention rates in colleges and universities. As retention in colleges and universities is of paramount concern in higher education, understanding the complex relationships among perfectionism, motivation, and maladaptive academic behaviors and outcomes will be an important avenue for future research.

CHAPTER 6

Future Directions for Academic Achievement and Perfectionism

Theoretical Model for Academic Achievement and Perfectionism

Based on the research reviewed in this book, a theoretical model has been developed that may serve as a guide for future research. We have recommended that potential moderator variables of parenting and personality must be examined in concert with potential mediator variables of motivation and academic maladjustment to fully explain the impact of perfectionism on academic achievement. Admittedly, long-term longitudinal studies starting in early childhood through adolescence are needed to completely determine the antecedents of perfectionism (Damian, Stoeber, Negru-Subtirica, & Baban, 2017; Hewitt, Flett, & Mikail, 2017). Yet research with undergraduate students and adults has provided empirical support for the relationships proposed in the theoretical model. Our theoretical framework for future research on perfectionism and academic achievement is presented in Figure 6.1. To explain the theoretical model, perfectionistic strivings and perfectionistic concerns will be examined separately.

Academic Achievement and Perfectionistic Strivings

Perfectionistic strivings seem to develop out of secure attachments to parents (Gnilka, Ashby, & Noble, 2013; Rice, Lopez, & Vergara, 2005; Rice & Mirzadeh, 2000) and authoritative parenting (Basirion, Majid, & Jelas, 2014; Dunkley, Berg, & Zuroff, 2012; Flett, Hewitt, & Singer, 1995; Sapieja, Dunn, & Hoit, 2011; Speirs Neumeister, 2004).

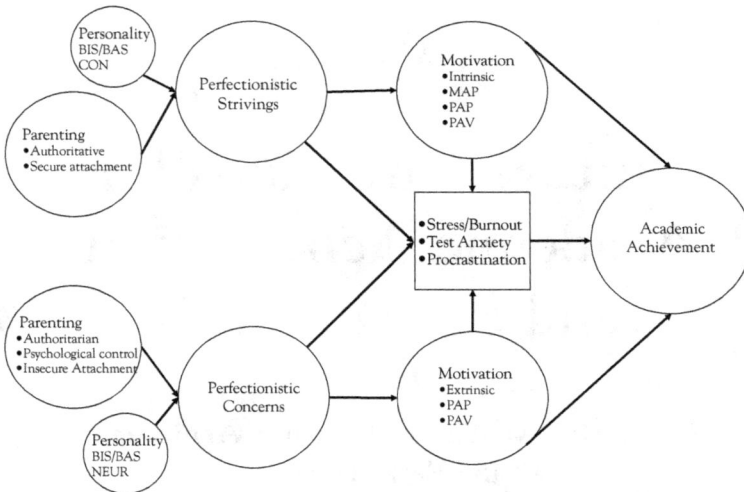

Figure 6.1 **Proposed theoretical model of mediators and moderators to explain the relationship between perfectionism and academic achievement.** BIS = Behavioral inhibition system; BAS = Behavioral activation system; CON = Conscientiousness; NEUR = Neuroticism; MAP = Mastery approach goals; PAP = Performance approach goals; PAV = Performance avoidance goals

Although research indicates that secure attachment and authoritative parenting are correlated (Karavasilis, Doyle, & Markiewicz, 2003; Speirs Neumeister & Finch, 2006), there are subtle differences in the two constructs: types of attachment status represent the emotionally quality and trust within the parent–child relationship (dependency) and authoritative parenting includes aspects of support for autonomy in children and adolescents (self). Drawing on the personality theories of Blatt (1974), the dichotomy between an individuals' preoccupation with others or preoccupation with the self is crucial for understanding the development of personality traits such as perfectionism. In short, authoritative parenting provides children and adolescents with autonomy support to explore their own interests, goals, and identity, allowing them to focus on the self, with little concern about harming their relationships with their parents or experiencing mean criticism and emotionally manipulative tactics (Rice et al., 2005).

Authoritative parenting and autonomy-supportive parenting have also been linked to positive motivational profiles in children and adolescents (Boon, 2007; Chen, 2015; Gonzalez & Wolters, 2006) and intrinsic, or autonomous, motivation (Bronstein, Ginsburg, & Herrera, 2005; Ginsburg & Bronstein, 1993; Grolnick & Ryan, 1989; Soenens & Vansteenkiste, 2005). Mastery approach goals and intrinsic motivation were positively associated with perfectionistic strivings (Bong, Hwang, Noh, & Kim, 2014; Damian, Stoeber, Negru, & Baban, 2014; Eum & Rice, 2011; Fletcher, Shim, & Wang, 2012; Gaudreau & Thompson, 2010; Miquelon et al., 2005; Stoeber, Feast, & Hayward, 2009; Speirs Neumeister & Finch, 2006; Van Yperen, 2006; Verner-Filion & Gaudreau, 2010). Yet perfectionistic strivings were also related to performance avoidance goals (Fletcher et al., 2012; Speirs Neumeister & Finch, 2006; Speirs Neumeister, Fletcher, & Burney, 2015; Van Yperen, 2006; Verner-Filion & Gaudreau, 2010). This motivational conflict related to goals for achievement (approach) and goals for avoiding failure (avoidance) likely increases the worry, rumination, and anxiety for students with perfectionistic strivings (Fletcher et al., 2012; Flett & Hewitt, 2006; Stoeber, 2014). Perhaps individuals with perfectionistic strivings may more frequently adopt adaptive motivations over maladaptive ones. For example, Verner-Filion and Gaudreau (2010) reported that individuals with high levels of perfectionistic strivings more often adopted performance approach goals over performance avoidance goals. Studies have shown that intrinsic motivation mediated the relationship between perfectionistic strivings (i.e., self-oriented) and academic adjustment (Miquelon et al., 2005) and performance approach goals mediated the positive relationship between perfectionistic strivings (i.e., self-oriented) and academic achievement (Vernon-Filion & Gaudreu, 2010).

Adopting an overall adaptive motivational profile may buffer students with perfectionistic strivings in times of academic stress, protecting them from potential academic burnout, test anxiety, and academic procrastination. There are several strands of empirical support that students with perfectionistic strivings may be protected from academic maladjustment: perfectionistic strivings were associated with less academic burnout (Chang, Lee, Byeon, & Lee, 2015; Chang, Lee, Byeon, Seong, & Lee, 2016; Hill & Curran, 2016; Shih, 2012), less test anxiety (Stoeber et al., 2009; Weiner & Carton, 2012), and less academic procrastination (Bong et al., 2014; Burnam, Komarraju, Hamel, & Nadler, 2014; Flett, Hewitt, & Martin, 1995; Ozer, O'Callaghan, Bokszczanin, Ederer, & Essau, 2014; Seo, 2008). In addition, perfectionistic strivings were associated with more engagement in academic studies (Damian et al., 2017; Shih, 2012; Shim, Rubenstein, & Drapeau, 2016; Zhang, Gan, & Cham, 2007).

One open research question, however, is the extent to which adaptive motivation may mediate the inverse relationships between perfectionistic strivings and academic maladjustment outcomes. Intrinsic motivation partially mediated the negative relationship between self-oriented perfectionism and academic burnout in two separate studies (Chang et al., 2015; Chang et al., 2016). Moreover, academic self-efficacy may also act as a potential mediator for the positive association between perfectionistic strivings and academic achievement (Bong et al., 2014; Flett, Hewitt, & Martin, 1995; Martin, Flett, Hewitt, Krames, & Szanto, 1996; Seo, 2008).

Perfectionistic strivings may arise from secure attachments with primary caregivers and authoritative parenting styles that foster autonomy and support for pursuing high achievement goals. Children within these supportive and caring relationships, in turn, may readily internalize messages about the importance of academics from their parents, leading to self-determined motivations focused on the self (intrinsic, mastery approach goals). Self-determined motivations then provide the necessary drive and stamina to work toward high levels of achievement, particularly in times of academic stress. However, we view the equilibrium between self-determined motivation and levels of academic stress as precarious: highly successful students with perfectionistic strivings might be able to navigate their academic work for many years before they experience academic stress or even academic failure. If successful students continue in their path toward higher education, academic failure will likely come. And at this point, perfectionistic reactivity (Flett & Hewitt, 2016) and dire predictions about how students with perfectionism may react to failure (Hall, 2016) will largely determine academic outcomes. Ask any faculty member that has worked with doctoral students and they are likely to have a story of a doctoral student that they observed *hit a wall*. In other words, students who were presented with negative feedback and criticism, perhaps for the first time in their academic career, and they completely shut down. Academic procrastination, fueled by fear of failure, may be particularly problematic as students with perfectionism move through higher levels of education, such as masters and doctoral degree programs (Onwuegbuzie, 2000). Observing and integrating how students with perfectionistic strivings react to academic failure will be a critical area of future research.

Academic Achievement and Perfectionistic Concerns

Perfectionistic concerns follow a different developmental pathway than perfectionistic strivings, with different precursors related to personality and parenting. Consistently, perfectionistic concerns were related to insecure attachments (Andersson & Perris, 2000; Dunkley et al., 2012; Rice & Lopez, 2004; Speirs Neumeister & Finch, 2006; Ulu & Tezer, 2010; Wei, Heppner, Russell, & Young, 2006) and authoritarian parenting (Basirion et al., 2014; Craddock, Church, & Sands, 2009; Flett et al.,1995; Gong, Fletcher, & Bolin, 2015; Hibbard & Walton, 2014; Kawamura, Frost, & Harmatz, 2002; Miller, Lambert, & Speirs Neumeister, 2012; Randolph & Dykman, 1996; Rice, Ashby, & Preusser, 1996; Speirs Neumeister, 2004). Individuals with perfectionistic concerns seem to endure parental criticism and harsh, competitive home environments focused on obeying parental authority at the expense of the students' own autonomy (Hutchinson & Yates, 2008; McArdle & Duda, 2004, 2008). Despite strong consistency in results across cross-sectional designs, in the only longitudinal study, parental criticism did not predict longitudinal increases in socially prescribed perfectionism (Damian, Stoeber, Negru, & Baban, 2013). Thus, longitudinal research is desperately needed to determine specific pathways of parental influence on perfectionism.

Considering the domain of academics, parents in the homes of students with perfectionistic concerns may have a hyper-focus on high academic achievement and superior academic achievement over others. To compel children to demonstrate superior academic achievement, parents may use psychological control such as withholding affection, shaming, and/or guilt trips to persuade their children to adopt their high achievement goals (Craddock et al, 2009; Fletcher et al, 2012; Shih, 2013; Soenens et al., 2005, 2008; Gong, Paulson, & Wang, 2016). Controlling parenting has been linked to maladaptive motivational profiles in children and adolescents (Chen, 2015; Gurland & Grolnick, 2005) and extrinsic motivation (Ginsburg & Bronstein, 1993). Perfectionism may even mediate the relationship between controlling parenting and students' motivation: concern over mistakes fully mediated the relationship between maternal psychological control and performance approach and performance avoidance goals (Fletcher et al., 2012). Similarly, in a sample of 15- to 17-year-old Israeli adolescents, parental criticism had a positive relationship with concern over mistakes and concern over mistakes predicted performance approach and performance avoidance goals (Madjar, Voltsis, & Weinstock, 2015).

Performance avoidance and extrinsic motivation were consistently associated with perfectionistic concerns (Bong et al., 2014; Damian et al., 2014; Eum & Rice, 2011; Fletcher et al., 2012; Hanchon, 2010; Speirs Neumeister et al., 2015; Gaudreau & Thompson, 2010; Mills & Blankstein, 2000; Miquelon et al., 2005; Stoeber et al., 2009; Speirs Neumeister & Finch, 2006; Vansteenkiste et al., 2010; Van Yperen, 2006; Verner-Filion & Gaudreau, 2010). Maladaptive patterns of motivation may mediate the relationships between perfectionistic concerns and measures of academic maladjustment: extrinsic motivation fully mediated the positive relationship between socially prescribed perfectionism and academic burnout in two separate studies (Chang et al., 2015; Chang et al., 2016). Furthermore, the relationship between perfectionistic concerns and test anxiety was mediated by performance avoidance goals in a sample of Korean middle school students (Bong et al., 2014).

Perfectionistic concerns, in combination with maladaptive achievement motivation, may increase the risk of students' negative academic adjustment, particularly under times of academic stress. Perfectionistic concerns were associated with higher academic stress (Rice, Richardson, & Ray, 2016), academic burnout (Chang et al., 2015; Chang et al., 2016; Hill & Curran, 2016; Shih, 2012), test anxiety (Bieling, Israeli, & Antony, 2004; Eum & Rice, 2011; Mills & Blankstein, 2000; Stoeber et al., 2009; Weiner & Carton, 2012), and academic procrastination (Bong et al., 2014; Burnam et al., 2014; Ozer et al., 2014; Rice, Richardson, & Clark, 2012). In addition, perfectionistic concerns were negatively associated with academic engagement (Shih, 2012); however, another study failed to find this relationship (Damian et al., 2017).

Perfectionistic concerns may arise from insecure attachments with primary caregivers and controlling parenting that fosters obedience and reduces children's autonomy. Children that develop perfectionistic concerns may also experience emotionally manipulative tactics from their parents. Children within these harsh and controlling relationships, in turn, may reject messages and resist internalizing their parents' expectations about academic achievement. Although students with perfectionistic concerns may be academically successful for extrinsic reasons such as praise and avoiding conflicts with their parents, they may never fully incorporate high value for academic achievement into their sense of self and are unlikely to experience joy and pride for their achievements. Academic achievement, for these students, may always be pursued for the aim of pleasing others and avoiding separation and rejection from important persons such as parents.

Without intrinsic motivations to support their efforts, students' perfectionistic concerns and maladaptive motivation will contribute to the development of dysfunctional attitudes and behaviors toward academic work such as burnout, anxiety, and procrastination. Academic evaluations are often stressful enough when undertaken for personal reasons. But imagine the additional layer of emotional exhaustion and anxiety experienced by individuals with perfectionistic concerns who are at risk of losing their emotional connection with parents and/or enduring personal attacks.

Directions for Future Research

Our theoretical model and literature review have provided multiple directions for future research to address specific research questions about perfectionism and its relationship to parenting, personality, achievement motivation, and academic behaviors. Moreover, we have argued that examining each of these constructs within the same longitudinal study starting in childhood into adolescence will provide empirical data to investigate the potential interactions and pathways for understanding the development of perfectionism and its consequences for academic achievement. Our hypotheses about how perfectionism contributes to academic achievement have drawn heavily from research that has focused on contexts and outcomes other than academic achievement. Finally, researchers of perfectionism must move toward including diverse students and families in studies related to academic achievement (Castro & Rice, 2003; DiBartolo & Rendon, 2012). In the last section, we have highlighted some areas of future research that may be particularly relevant in the academic context.

School Professionals and Perfectionism in the Academic Context

Although our review focused on how parents influence perfectionism (see Chapter 3), Flett, Hewitt, Oliver, and Macdonald (2002) also included teachers and peers as potential environmental influences on the development of perfectionism. Teachers are prominent influences on students' academic achievement and as such, they might also contribute to students' perfectionistic tendencies. Much like parents, teachers give emotional support and direct messages related to academic expectations and achievement motivations in their classrooms (see Wentzel, 2009 for a review). To our knowledge, however, there has been very little research on how teachers' classroom behavior might impact students' perfectionism (Shih, 2013). In addition to teachers, peer influences on academic achievement have been documented: when students moved to a peer group with higher academic achievement, they experienced an increase in grades (Mounts & Steinberg, 1995). Peer relationships and the impact on students' perfectionism in school has received limited research attention (Gilman, Adams, & Nounopoulos, 2011; Lyman & Luthar, 2014). Moreover, peer and teacher influences on perfectionism may interact with culture: Asian-American undergraduates' socially prescribed perfectionism was related to pressures from teachers, friends, and peers to be perfect, whereas only pressure to be perfect from teachers was related to European American undergraduates' socially prescribed perfectionism (Perera & Chang, 2015).

Despite a few studies on perfectionism and peers, none examined how the dynamics among members of the peer groups might contribute to students' perfectionistic tendencies, and in turn, impact academic achievement. But it is not hard to see how perfectionistic traits about academic work within a peer group, particularly expressed by the leader of the group, may also spread to other students. In addition to teachers and peers, Appleton and Curran (2016) recently argued that coaches and instructors influence the development of perfectionistic traits. Coaches, peers, and teachers, in different contexts, set the tone for achievement expectations and the content of motivational messages (e.g., mastery vs. performance) as adolescents are establishing autonomy from their parents. Understanding the mechanisms of how other professionals in schools such as coaches and teachers influence students' perfectionism, beyond parental influences, will require much more research.

Individual Differences and Perfectionism in the Academic Context

In addition to different types of professionals working with students in academic settings, individual differences among students may also be associated with different levels and/or types of perfectionism. Perfectionism in gifted students has been widely examined for decades (see Speirs Neumeister, 2017 for a review), yet we know little about perfectionism and students with disabilities such as attention deficit hyperactivity disorder (ADHD), learning disabilities (LD), and autism spectrum disorder (ASD), to name a few. Students in each of these classifications suffer from deficits in executive functioning skills. Executive functioning skills include attention shifting, working memory, and controlling impulses. Research has found that executive functioning, in combination with a fearful temperament, predicted children's perfectionistic concerns (Affrunti & Woodruff-Borden, 2016). In a longitudinal study of African-American students from first grade to sixth grade, students who were eventually classified as critical perfectionists (i.e., higher perfectionistic concerns) in the sixth grade had higher levels of inattention and hyperactivity problems compared with the students in the other perfectionist groups (Herman, Trotter, Reinke, & Ialongo, 2011). Albeit quite preliminary, the study of interactions between perfectionism and executive functioning in children and adolescents warrants research attention. Theoretical models of perfectionism in adults have incorporated aspects of self-regulation (Sirois, 2016) and emotional regulation (Richardson, Rice, & Devine, 2014). To our knowledge, there has been little work conducted to examine perfectionistic tendencies in students with disabilities who might have executive function deficits (Greenaway & Howlin, 2010). If perfectionistic concerns are hindering students with disabilities from reaching their full achievement potential, much more research is needed and should involve professionals in different disciplines such as special education and school psychology.

Challenge and Perfectionism in the Academic Context

One upsetting potential outcome of perfectionism on academic achievement may be students' resistance to seeking academic challenge in the form of advanced coursework in high school and college. How many intellectually able students shun enrolling in Advanced Placement (AP) courses in high school because they are afraid of performing less than perfectly? In higher education, what role does perfectionism play in undergraduates' decisions about whether to enroll in a study abroad or competitive internship program? Based on our literature review, we have hypothesized that students with perfectionistic strivings might be able to offset avoidance tendencies, or at least to counterbalance with approach tendencies, to seek positive fulfillment of achievement from academic challenges. In contrast, potential failure from academic challenges would be the dominant concern for students with perfectionistic concerns and avoidance tendencies. Who knows how many competent students resist academic opportunities that would greatly contribute to their growth as a student due to their fear of failure? Research is needed to determine how perfectionism and avoidance motivations contribute to decisions about taking on challenging academic work.

But once students make a decision to accept demanding academic work, perfectionism may also impact how they may respond to failure or less than perfect performance (Hewitt & Flett, 1993; Hewitt, Flett, & Ediger, 1996). In the sports domain, Flett and Hewitt (2016) described the concept of perfectionistic reactivity—"a characteristic style of responding to adversity that includes both psychological reactivity and physiological reactivity" (p. 301). In other words, individuals with perfectionism will react intensely to situations where they realize that they are unlikely to perform perfectly. Recent commentaries about the future directions of perfectionism research in the area of sports psychology by Hall (2016) and Flett and Hewitt have called for an analysis of how perfectionists react to failure and its effect on their motivation. When some individuals with perfectionism encounter potential failure or even the threat of failure, approach motivations may override their fear of failure and propel them toward their goals. According to Hall and Flett and Hewitt, however, individuals with high levels of perfectionism who are able to stay focused on reaching their goals in the face of failure are likely uncommon. More likely, ruminations and worry about setbacks and failures will stall progress toward their goals and come at the cost of worry, rumination, self-criticism, and anxiety, particularly for those perfectionists who have high levels of perfectionistic concerns. Researchers have created ways to study perfectionism by inducing failure and stress in research paradigms (Altstötter-Gleich, Gerstenberg, & Brand, 2012; DiBartolo & Varner, 2012; Stoeber, Hutchfield, & Wood, 2008; Stoeber, Kempe, & Keogh, 2008). However, research should be designed to investigate perfectionists' cumulative reactions to success and failure in natural settings such as semester long coursework or internships, adding additional variables related to adaptive and maladaptive motivation. Studies attending to these considerations will greatly contribute to the understanding of how perfectionism and academic achievement are influenced by motivational forces. Interactions among perfectionistic strivings, perfectionistic concerns, and academic challenge are an area of critical future research.

Multidisciplinary Research and Perfectionism

The literature is replete with studies suggesting that individuals with high levels of perfectionism may also experience higher levels of psychopathology including depression, stress, anxiety, and eating disorders (see Limburg, Watson, Hagger, & Egan, 2016 for a recent meta-analysis). For some children and adolescents with perfectionism battling depression, anxiety, and eating disorders at the clinical level, concerns about academic achievement are likely to be minimal. However, many students that have been diagnosed with psychological disorders and/or may suffer from elevated levels of symptoms related to depression and anxiety also must deal with academic requirements. Conversely, academic requirements and stress may lead to elevated symptoms of anxiety and depression. What are the unique contributions of perfectionism, psychological adjustment, and academic adjustment to academic achievement? The work of Keith Herman and colleagues (2011, 2013), which has examined the developmental precursors and pathways for perfectionism using both psychological and academic outcomes in a sample of urban, African-American students, serves as a model for future research in other populations. Multidisciplinary research involving clinical psychologists, school psychologists, and educational psychologists will need to be conducted. Researchers in different disciplines need to join forces to examine how individuals with perfectionism cope and deal with this personality trait across different life domains.

Conclusion

The proposed theoretical model of perfectionism and academic achievement, as well as areas such as individual differences among students, the influence of other professionals in schools, and students' reactions to academic challenge, provide students and faculty with recommendations for future research. It is our hope that this theoretical model has outlined a blueprint for advanced students and their faculty mentors to expand upon previous work on perfectionism and academic achievement. Much more research is needed to explain the effects of perfectionism on academic achievement. With additional research on perfectionism and academic achievement, school professionals may move toward ways to target students with perfectionistic concerns and intervene early in their school years, possibly saving them from years of stress and anxiety. School professionals should also be concerned with students with perfectionistic strivings: they will need support and monitoring as they approach academic challenges that might overwhelm their coping resources. Prevention and intervention efforts that more effectively target aspects of perfectionism that are problematic, such as challenge and potential failure, will allow students to achieve in accordance with their potential.

References

Abdollahi, A., & Talib, M. A. (2015). Emotional intelligence moderates perfectionism and test anxiety among Iranian students. *School Psychology International, 36*(5), 498–512.

Adler, A. (1956). *The individual psychology of Alfred Adler: A systematic presentation in selections from his writings.* In H. L. Ansbacher & R. R. Ansbacher (Eds.), New York: Basic Books.

Affrunti, N. W., Gramszlo, C., & Woodruff-Borden, J. (2016). Executive function moderates the association between fearful temperament and dimensions of perfectionism. *Personality and Individual Differences, 89*, 117–122.

Affrunti, N. W., & Woodruff-Borden, J. (2015). Parental perfectionism and overcontrol: Examining mechanisms in the development of child anxiety. *Journal of Abnormal Child Psychology, 43*(3), 517–529. doi:10.1007/s10802-014-9914-5

Ainsworth, M. (1989). Attachments beyond infancy. *American Psychologist, 44*(4), 709–716.

Altstötter-Gleich, C., Gerstenberg, F. X. R., & Brand, M. (2012). Performing well—Feeling bad? Effects of perfectionism under experimentally induced stress on tension and performance. *Journal of Research in Personality, 46*(5), 619–622.

Amabile, T. M., Hill, K. G., Hennessey, B. A., & Tighe, E. M. (1994). The Work Preference Inventory: Assessing intrinsic and extrinsic motivational orientations. *Journal of Personality and Social Psychology, 66*(5), 950–967.

Andersson, P., & Perris, C. (2000). Attachment styles and dysfunctional assumptions in adults. *Clinical Psychology and Psychotherapy, 7*(1), 47–53.

Appleton, P. R., & Curran, T. (2016). The origins of perfectionism in sport, dance, and exercise. In A. P. Hill, (Ed.), *The psychology of perfectionism in sport, dance and exercise* (pp. 57–81). New York: Routledge/Taylor & Francis Group.

Appleton, P., Hall, H., & Hill, A. (2010). Family patterns of perfectionism: an examination of elite junior athletes and their parents. *Psychology of Sport and Exercise, 11*(5), 363–371.

Arana, F. G., & Furlan, L. (2016). Groups of perfectionists, test anxiety, and pre-exam coping in Argentine students. *Personality and Individual Differences, 90*, 169–173.

Aupperle, R. L., & Paulus, M. P. (2010). Neural systems underlying approach and avoidance in anxiety disorders. *Dialogues in Clinical Neuroscience, 12*(4), 305–319.

Bach, D. R., Guitart-Masip, M., Packard, P. A., Miró, J., Falip, M., Fuentemilla, L., & Dolan, R. J. (2014). Human hippocampus arbitrates approach-avoidance conflict. *Current Biology, 24*(5), 541–547.

Bandura, A. (1977). Self-efficacy: Toward a unifying theory of behavioral change. *Psychological Review, 84*(2), 191–215.

Bandura, A. (1986). Fearful expectations and avoidant actions as coeffects of perceived self-inefficacy. *American Psychologist, 41*(12), 1389–1391.

Barber, B. K. (1996). Parental psychological control: Revising a neglected construct. *Child Development, 67*(6), 3296–3319.

Bartholomew, K., & Horowitz, L. M. (1991). Attachment styles among young adults: A test of a four-category model. *Journal of Personality and Social Psychology, 61*(2), 226–244.

Basirion, Z., Majid, R. A., & Jelas, Z. M. (2014). Big Five personality factors, perceived parenting styles, and perfectionism among academically gifted students. *Asian Social Science, 10*(4), 8–15.

Baumrind, D. H. (1971). Current patterns of parental authority. *Developmental Psychology Monographs, 4*(1p2), 1–103.

Bieling, P., Israeli, A. L., & Antony, M. M. (2004). Is perfectionism good, bad, or both? Examining models of the perfectionism construct. *Personality and Individual Differences, 36*(6), 1373–1385.

Bieling, P. J., Israeli, A., Smith, J., & Anthony, M. M. (2003). Making the grade: the behavioral consequences of perfectionism in the classroom. *Personality and Individual Differences, 35*(1), 163–178.

Blankstein, K. R., Dunkley, D. M., & Wilson, J. (2008). Evaluative concerns and personal standards perfectionism: Self-esteem as a mediator and moderator of relations with personal and academic needs and estimated GPA. *Current Psychology: A Journal for Diverse Perspectives on Diverse Psychological Issues, 27*(1), 29–61.

Blatt, S. J. (1974). Levels of object representation in anaclitic and introjective depression. *The Psychoanalytic Study of the Child, 29*, 107–157. New Haven, CT: Yale University Press.

Blatt, S. J. (2004). *Experience of depression: Theoretical, clinical and research perspectives*. Washington, DC: American Psychological Association.

Blatt, S. J., D'Afflitti, J. P., & Quinlan, D. M. (1976). *Depressive experiences questionnaire*. New Haven, CT: Yale University Press.

Blatt, S. J., & Levy, K. N. (2003). Attachment theory, psychoanalysis, personality development and psychopathology. *Psychoanalytic Inquiry, 23*(1), 104–152.

Blatt, S. J., & Luyten, P. (2009). A structural-developmental psychodynamic approach to psychopathology: Two polarities of experience across the life span. *Development and Psychopathology, 21*(3), 793–814.

Blatt, S. J., & Zuroff, D. C. (1992). Interpersonal relatedness and self-definition: Two prototypes for depression. *Clinical Psychology Review, 12*(5), 527–562.

Bleys, D., Soenens, B., Boone, L., Claes, S., Vliegen, N., & Luyten, P. (2016). The role of intergenerational similarity and parenting in adolescent self-criticism: An actor–partner interdependence model. *Journal of Adolescence, 49*, 68–76.

Blunt, A. K., & Pychyl, T. A. (2000). Task aversiveness and procrastination: A multi-dimensional approach to task aversiveness across stages of personal projects. *Personality and Individual Differences, 28*(1), 153–167.

Bong, M., Hwang, A., Noh, A., & Kim, S. (2014). Perfectionism and motivation of adolescents in academic contexts. *Journal of Educational Psychology, 106*(3), 711–729.

Boon, H. J. (2007). Low- and high-achieving Australian secondary school students: Their parenting, motivations and academic achievement. *Australian Psychologist, 42*(3), 212–225.

Bowlby, J. (1980). *Attachment and loss: Sadness and depression* (Vol. 3). New York, NY: Basic Books.

Bowlby, J. (1988). *A secure base.* New York, NY: Basic Books.

Brennan, K. A., Clark, C. L., & Shaver, P. R. (1998). Self-report measurement of adult attachment: An integrative overview. In J. A. Simpson & W. S. Rholes (Eds.), *Attachment theory and close relationships* (pp. 46–76). New York, NY: Guilford Press.

Bronstein, P., Ginsburg, G. S., & Herrera, I. S. (2005). Parental predictors of motivational orientation in early adolescence: A longitudinal study. *Journal of Youth and Adolescence, 34*(6), 559–575.

Brown, E. J., Heimberg, R. G., Frost, R. O., Makris, G. S., Juster, H. R., & Leung, A. W. (1999). Relationship of perfectionism to affect, expectations, attributions and performance in the classroom. *Journal of Social and Clinical Psychology, 18*(1), 98–120.

Brownlow, S., & Reasinger, R. D. (2000). Putting off until tomorrow what is better done today: Academic procrastination as a function of motivation toward college work. *Journal of Social Behavior and Personality, 15*(5), 15–34.

Buri J. R. (1991). Parental authority questionnaire. *Journal of Personality Assessment, 57*, 110–119.

Burnam, A., Komarraju, M., Hamel, R., & Nadler D. R. (2014). Do adaptive perfectionism and self-determined motivation reduce academic procrastination? *Learning and Individual Differences, 36*, 165–172.

Burns, D. D. (1980). The perfectionist's script for self-defeat. *Psychology Today, 14*(6), 34–52.

Burns, L. R., Dittmann, K., Nguyen, N., & Mitchelson, J. K. (2000). Academic procrastination, perfectionism, and control: Associations with vigilant and avoidant coping. *Journal of Social Behavior and Personality, 15*(5), 35–46.

Carver, C. S., & White, T. L. (1994). Behavioral inhibition, behavioral activation, and affective responses to impending reward and punishment: The BIS/BAS Scales. *Journal of Personality and Social Psychology, 67*(2), 319–333.

Cassady, J. C. (2004). The influence of cognitive test anxiety across the learning-testing cycle. *Learning and Instruction, 14*(6), 569–592.

Cassady, J. C. (2010). Test anxiety: Contemporary theories and implications for learning. In J. C. Cassady, (Ed.), *Anxieties in schools: The causes, consequences, and solutions for academic anxieties* (pp. 5–26). New York, NY: Peter Lang.

Cassady, J. C., & Johnson, R. E. (2002). Cognitive test anxiety and academic performance. *Contemporary Educational Psychology, 27*(2), 270–295.

Castro, J. R., & Rice, K. G. (2003). Perfectionism and ethnicity: Implications for depressive symptoms and self-reported academic achievement. *Cultural Diversity and Ethnic Minority Psychology, 9*(1), 64–78.

Chang, E. C., Lee, A., Byeon, E., & Lee, S. M. (2015). Role of motivation in the relation between perfectionism and academic burnout in Korean students. *Personality and Individual Differences, 82*, 221–226.

Chang, E., Lee, A., Byeon, E., Seong, H., & Lee, S. M. (2016). The mediating effect of motivational types in the relationship between perfectionism and academic burnout. *Personality and Individual Differences, 89*, 202–210.

Chang, E. C., Zumberg, K. M., Sanna, L. J., Girz, L. P., Kade, A. M., Shair, S. R., Hermann, N. B., & Srivastava, K. (2007). Relationship between perfectionism and domains of worry in a college student population: Considering the role of BIS/BAS motives. *Personality and Individual Differences, 43*(4), 925–936.

Chapell, M. S., Blanding, Z. B., Silverstein, M. E., Takahashi, M., Newman, B., Gubi, A., & McCann, N. (2005). Test anxiety and academic performance in undergraduate and graduate students. *Journal of Educational Psychology, 97*(2), 268–274.

Chen, W. (2015). The relations between perceived parenting styles and academic achievement in Hong Kong: The mediating role of students' goal orientations. *Learning and Individual Differences, 37*, 48–54.

Chen, C., Hewitt, P., & Flett, G. (2015). Preoccupied attachment, need to belong, shame, and interpersonal perfectionism: An investigation of the Perfectionism Social Disconnection Model. *Personality and Individual Differences, 76*, 177–182.

Chen, C., Hewitt, P. L., Flett, G. L., Birch, S., Cassels, T. G., & Blasberg, J. S. (2012). Insecure attachment, perfectionistic self-presentation, and social disconnection in adolescents. *Personality and Individual Differences, 52*(8), 936–941.

Church, M. A., Elliot, A. J., & Gable, S. L. (2001). Perceptions of classroom environment, achievement goals, and achievement outcomes. *Journal of Educational Psychology, 93*(1), 43–54.

Clark, S., & Coker, S. (2009). Perfectionism, self-criticism and maternal criticism: A study of mothers and their children. *Personality and Individual Differences, 47*(4), 321–325.

Collins, N. L., & Read, S. J. (1990). Adult attachment, working models, and relationship quality in dating couples. *Journal of Personality and Social Psychology, 58*(4), 644–663.

Cook, L. C., & Kearney, C. A. (2009). Parent and youth perfectionism and internalizing psychopathology. *Personality and Individual Differences, 46*(3), 325–330.

Cook, L. C., & Kearney, C. A. (2014). Parent perfectionism and psychopathology symptoms and child perfectionism. *Personality and Individual Differences, 70,* 1–6.

Corr, P. J., & Cooper, A. J. (2016). The Reinforcement Sensitivity Theory of Personality Questionnaire (RST-PQ): Development and validation. *Psychological Assessment, 28*(11), 1427–1440.

Costa, P. T., & McCrae, R. R. (1992). *Revised NEO Personality Inventory* (NEO-PI-R). Odessa, FL: Psychological Assessment Resources.

Costa, P., & McCrae, R. (1995). Domains and facets: Hierarchical personality assessment using the Revised NEO Personality Inventory. *Journal of Personality Assessment, 64*(1), 21–50.

Cox, B. J., Enns, M. W., & Clara, I. P. (2002). The multidimensional structure of perfectionism in clinically distressed and college student samples. *Psychological Assessment, 14*(3), 365–373.

Craddock, A. E., Church, W., & Sands, A. (2009). Family of origin characteristics as predictors of perfectionism. *Australian Journal of Psychology, 61*(3), 136–144.

Crowell, J. A., Fraley, R. C., & Shaver, P. R. (1999). Measurement of individual differences in adolescent and adult attachment. In J. Cassidy & P. R. Shaver (Eds.), *Handbook of attachment: Theory, research, and clinical applications* (pp. 434–465). New York: The Guilford Press.

Cruce, S. E., Pashak, T. J., Handal, P. J., Munz, D. C., & Gfeller, J. D. (2012). Conscientious perfectionism, self-evaluative perfectionism, and the five-factor model of personality traits. *Personality and Individual Differences, 53*(3), 268–273.

Dabrowski, K. (1964). *Positive disintegration.* Oxford, England: Little, Brown.

Damian, L. E., Stoeber, J., Negru, O., & Băban, A. (2013). On the development of perfectionism in adolescence: Perceived parental expectations predict longitudinal increases in socially prescribed perfectionism. *Personality and Individual Differences, 55*(6), 688–693.

Damian, L., Stoeber, J., Negru, O., & Băban, A. (2014). Perfectionism and achievement goal orientations in adolescent school students. *Psychology in the Schools, 51*(9), 960–971. doi:10.1002/pits.21794

Damian, L. E., Stoeber, J., Negru-Subtirica, O., & Băban, A. (2016). On the development of perfectionism: The longitudinal role of academic achievement and academic efficacy. *Journal of Personality*. doi:10.1111/jopy.12261

Damian, L. E., Stoeber, J., Negru-Subtirica, O., & Băban, A. (2017). Perfectionism and school engagement: A three-wave longitudinal study. *Personality and Individual Differences, 105*, 179–184.

Deci, E. L., & Ryan, R. M. (2000). The 'what' and 'why' of goal pursuits: Human needs and the self-determination of behavior. *Psychological Inquiry, 11*(4), 227–268.

DeCuyper, K., Claes, L., Hermans, D., Pieters, G., & Smits, D. (2015). Psychometric properties of the Multidimensional Perfectionism Scale of Hewitt in a Dutch-speaking sample: Associations with the Big Five personality traits. *Journal of Personality Assessment, 97*(2), 182–190.

DiBartolo, P. M., & Rendón, M. J. (2012). A critical examination of the construct of perfectionism and its relationship to mental health in Asian and African Americans using a cross-cultural framework. *Clinical Psychology Review, 32*(3), 139–152.

DiBartolo, P. M., & Varner, S. P. J. (2012). How children's cognitive and affective responses to a novel task relate to the dimensions of perfectionism. *Journal of Rational-Emotive and Cognitive-Behavior Therapy, 30*(2), 62–76.

Dunkley, D. M., Berg, J., & Zuroff, D. (2012). The role of perfectionism in daily self-esteem, attachment, and negative affect. *Journal of Personality, 80*(3), 633–663.

Dunkley, D. M., Blankstein, K. R., & Berg, J. L. (2012). Perfectionism dimensions and the five-factor model of personality. *European Journal of Personality, 26*(3), 233–244.

Dunkley, D. M., Blankstein, K. R., Zuroff, D. C., Lecce, S., & Hui, D. (2006). Self-Critical and Personal Standards factors of perfectionism located within the five-factor model of personality. *Personality and Individual Differences, 40*(3), 409–420.

Dunkley, D. M., & Kyparissis, A. (2008). What is DAS self-critical perfectionism really measuring? Relations with the five-factor model of personality and depressive symptoms. *Personality and Individual Differences, 44*(6), 1295–1305.

Dunkley, D. M., Zuroff, D. C., & Blankstein, K. R. (2003). Self-critical perfectionism and daily affect: Dispositional and situational influences on stress and coping. *Journal Of Personality and Social Psychology, 84*(1), 234–252.

Dunkley, D. M., Zuroff, D. C., & Blankstein, K. R. (2006). Specific perfectionism components versus self-criticism in predicting maladjustment. *Personality and Individual Differences, 40*(4), 665–676.

Dunn, J. H., Dunn, J. C., & McDonald, K. (2012). Domain-specific perfectionism in intercollegiate athletes: Relationships with perceived competence and perceived importance in sport and school. *Psychology of Sport And Exercise, 13*(6), 747–755.

Dunn, J. H., Gotwals, J. K., & Dunn, J. C. (2005). An examination of the domain specificity of perfectionism among intercollegiate student-athletes. *Personality and Individual Differences, 38*(6), 1439–1448. doi:10.1016/j.paid.2004.09.009

Egan, S. J., Vinciguerra, T., & Mazzucchelli, T. G. (2015). The role of perfectionism, agreeableness, and neuroticism in predicting dyadic adjustment. *Australian Journal of Psychology, 67*(1), 1–9.

Egan, S. J., Wade, T. D., & Shafran, R. (2011). Perfectionism as a transdiagnostic process: A clinical review. *Clinical Psychology Review, 31*(2), 203–212.

Elion, A. A., Wang, K. T., Slaney, R. B., & French, B. H. (2012). Perfectionism in African American students: Relationship to racial identity, GPA, self-esteem, and depression. *Cultural Diversity and Ethnic Minority Psychology, 18*(2), 118–127.

Elliot, A. J. (1997). Integrating the "classic" and "contemporary" approaches to achievement motivation: A hierarchical model of approach and avoidance achievement motivation. In M. Maehr & P. Pintrich (Eds.), *Advances in motivation and achievement* (Vol. 10, pp. 243–279). Greenwich, CT: JAI Press.

Elliot, A. J. (2005). A conceptual history of the achievement goal construct. In A. J. Elliot & C. S. Dweck (Eds.), *Handbook of competence and motivation* (pp. 52–72). New York, NY: Guilford Publications.

Elliot, A. J., & Church, M. A. (1997). A hierarchical model of approach and avoidance achievement motivation. *Journal of Personality and Social Psychology, 72*(1), 218–232.

Elliot, A. J., & McGregor, H. A. (1999). Test anxiety and the hierarchical model of approach and avoidance achievement motivation. *Journal of Personality and Social Psychology, 76*(4), 628–644.

Elliot, A. J., & McGregor, H. A. (2001). A 2×2 achievement goal framework. *Journal of Personality and Social Psychology, 80*(3), 501–519.

Elliot, A. J., Murayama, K., & Pekrun, R. (2011). A 3 × 2 achievement goal model. *Journal of Educational Psychology, 103*(3), 632–648.

Enns, M. W., Cox, B. J., & Clara, I. (2002). Adaptive and maladaptive perfectionism: Developmental origins and association with depression proneness. *Personality and Individual Differences, 33*(6), 921–935.

Eum, K., & Rice, K. G. (2011). Text anxiety, perfectionism, goal orientation, and academic performance. *Anxiety, Stress, and Coping, 24*(2), 167–178.

Ferrari, J. R., & Sapadin, L. (2014). Procrastination. In L. Grossman & S. Walfish (Eds.), *Translating psychological research into practice* (pp. 241–246). New York, NY: Springer Publishing Co.

Fletcher, K. L., Shim, S. S., & Wang, C. (2012). Perfectionistic concerns mediate the relationship between psychologically controlling parenting and achievement goal orientations. *Personality and Individual Differences, 52*(8), 876–881.

Fletcher, K. L., & Speirs Neumeister, K. L. (2012). Research on perfectionism and achievement motivation: Implications for gifted students. *Psychology in the Schools, 49*(7), 668–677.

Flett, G. L., Blankstein, K., & Hewitt, P. (2009). Perfectionism, performance, and state positive affect and negative affect after a classroom test. *Canadian Journal of School Psychology, 24*(1), 4–18.

Flett, G. L., Blankstein, K. R., Hewitt, P. L., & Koledin, S. (1992). Components of perfectionism and procrastination in college students. *Social Behavior and Personality, 20*(2), 85–94.

Flett, G. L., Druckman, T., Hewitt, P. L., & Wekerle, C. (2012). Perfectionism, coping, social support, and depression in maltreated adolescents. *Journal of Rational-Emotive & Cognitive-Behavior Therapy, 30*(2), 118–131.

Flett, G. L., & Hewitt, P. L. (2002). *Perfectionism: Theory, research and treatment.* New York: American Psychological Association.

Flett, G. L., & Hewitt, P. L. (2005). The perils of perfectionism in sports and exercise. *Current Directions in Psychological Science, 14*(1), 14–18.

Flett, G. L., & Hewitt, P. L. (2006). Positive versus negative perfectionism in psychopathology: A comment on Slade and Owens's Dual Process Model. *Behavior Modification, 30*(4), 472–495.

Flett, G. L., & Hewitt, P. L. (2013). Disguised distress in children and adolescents "Flying under the radar": Why psychological problems are underestimated and how schools must respond. *Canadian Journal of School Psychology, 28*(1), 1–16.

Flett, G. L., & Hewitt, P. L. (2014). "The perils of perfectionism in sports" revisited: Toward a broader understanding of the pressure to be perfect and its impact on athletes and dancers. *International Journal of Sport Psychology, 45*(4), 395–407.

Flett, G. L., & Hewitt, P. L. (2016). Reflections on perfection and pressure to be perfect in athletes, dancers, and exercisers: A focus on perfectionistic reactivity in key situations and life contexts. In A. P. Hill, (Ed.), *The psychology of perfectionism in sport, dance and exercise* (pp. 296–315). New York, NY: Routledge/Taylor & Francis Group.

Flett, G. L., Hewitt, P. L., Boucher, D. J., Davidson, L. A., & Munro, Y. (1997). The Child and Adolescent Perfectionism Scale: Development, validation and association with adjustment. Unpublished manuscript, York University, Toronto, Ontario, Canada.

Flett, G. L., Hewitt, P. L., Davis, R. A., & Sherry, S. B. (2004). Description and counseling of the Perfectionistic Procrastinator. In H. C. Schouwenburg, C. H. Lay, T. A. Pychyl, & J. R. Ferrari (Eds.), *Counseling the procrastinator in academic settings* (pp. 181–194). Washington, DC: American Psychological Association.

Flett, G. L., Hewitt, P. L., & Martin, T. R. (1995). Dimensions of perfectionism and procrastination. In *Procrastination and task avoidance: Theory, research, and treatment* (pp. 113–136). New York, NY: Plenum Press.

Flett, G. L., Hewitt, P. L., Oliver, J. M., & Macdonald, S. (2002). Perfectionism in children and their parents: A developmental analysis. In G. L. Flett, & P. L. Hewitt (Eds.), *Perfectionism: Theory, research, and treatment* (pp. 89–132). Washington, DC: American Psychological Association.

Flett, G. L., Hewitt, P. L., & Singer, A. (1995). Perfectionism and parental authority styles. *Individual Psychology: Journal of Adlerian Theory, Research & Practice, 51*(1), 50–60.

Franche, V., & Gaudreau, P. (2016). Integrating dispositional perfectionism and within-person variations of perfectionism across life domains into a multilevel extension of the 2 × 2 model of perfectionism. *Personality and Individual Differences, 89*, 55–59.

Franche, V., Gaudreau, P., & Miranda, D. (2012). The 2×2 model of perfectionism: A comparison across Asian Canadians and European Canadians. *Journal of Counseling Psychology, 59*(4), 567–574.

Fredricks, J. A., Blumenfeld, P., Friedel, J., & Paris, A. (2005). "School engagement." In K. A. Moore, & L. H. Lippman, (Eds.), *What do children need to flourish: Conceptualizing and measuring indicators of positive development* (pp. 305–321). New York, NY: Springer Science+Business Media.

Frost, R. 0., Heimberg, R. G., Holt, C. S., Mattia,. I., & Neubauer, A. L. (1993). A comparison of two measures of perfectionism. *Personality and Individual Differences, 14*(1), 119–126.

Frost, R. O., Lahart, C. M., & Rosenblate, R. (1991). The development of perfectionism: A study of daughters and their parents. *Cognitive Therapy and Research, 15*(6), 469–489.

Frost, R. O., Marten, P., Lahart, C. M., & Rosenblate, R. (1990). The dimensions of perfectionism. *Cognitive Therapy and Research, 14*(5), 449–468.

Frost, R. O., Turcotte, T. A., Heimberg, R. G., Mattia, J. I., Holt, C. S., & Hope, D. A. (1995). Reactions to mistakes among subjects high and low in perfectionistic concern over mistakes. *Cognitive Therapy and Research, 19*(2), 195–205.

Gaudreau, P. (2012). A methodological note on the interactive and main effects of dualistic personality dimensions: An example using the 2×2 model of perfectionism. *Personality and Individual Differences, 52*, 26–31.

Gaudreau, P., & Antl, S. (2008). Athletes' broad dimensions of dispositional perfectionism: Examining changes in life satisfaction and the mediating role of sport-related motivation and coping. *Journal of Sport and Exercise Psychology, 30*(3), 356–382.

Gaudreau, P., Franche, V., & Gareau, A. (2016). A latent mediated moderation of perfectionism, motivation, and academic satisfaction: Advancing the 2×2 model of perfectionism through substantive-methodological synergy. *Journal of Psychoeducational Assessment, 34*(7), 688–701.

Gaudreau, P., & Thompson, A. (2010). Testing a 2×2 model of dispositional perfectionism. *Personality and Individual Differences, 48*(5), 532–537.

Gilman, R., Adams, R., & Nounopoulos, A. (2011). The interpersonal relationships and social perceptions of adolescent perfectionists. *Journal of Research on Adolescence, 21*(2), 505–511.

Gioia, G. A., Isquith, P. K., Guy, S. C., & Kenworthy, L. (2000). *Behavior rating inventory of executive function*. Lutz, FL: Psychological Assessment Resources.

Ginsburg, G. S., & Bronstein, P. (1993). Family factors related to children's intrinsic/extrinsic motivational orientation and academic performance. *Child Development, 64*(5), 1461–1474.

Gnilka, P., Ashby, J., & Noble, C. (2013). Adaptive and maladaptive perfectionism as mediators of adult attachment styles and depression, hopelessness, and life satisfaction. *Journal of Counseling and Development, 91*(1), 78–86.

Goldberg, D. P., & Hillier, V. F. (1979). A scaled version of the General Health Questionnaire. *Psychological Medicine, 9*(1), 139–145.

Gong, X., Fletcher, K. L., & Bolin, J. H. (2015). Dimensions of perfectionism mediate the relationship between parenting styles and coping. *Journal of Counseling and Development, 93*(3), 259–268.

Gong, X., Paulson, S. E., & Wang, C. (2016). Exploring family origins of perfectionism: The impact of interparental conflict and parenting behaviors. *Personality and Individual Differences, 100*, 43–48.

Gonzalez, A., & Wolters, C. A. (2006). The relation between perceived parenting practices and achievement motivation in mathematics. *Journal of Research in Childhood Education, 21*(2), 203–217.

Gotwals, J. K. (2016). The tripartite model of perfectionism: Evidence from research in sport and dance. In A. P. Hill, (Ed.), *The psychology of perfectionism in sport, dance and exercise* (pp. 150–173). New York, NY: Routledge/Taylor & Francis Group.

Gotwals, J. K., & Dunn, J. G. H. (2009). A multi-method multi-analytic approach to establishing internal construct validity evidence: The Sport Multidimensional Perfectionism Scale 2. *Measurement in Physical Education and Exercise Science, 13*(2), 71–92.

Gray, J. A. (1991). Neural systems of motivation, emotion, and affect. In J. Madden (Ed.), *Neurobiology of learning, emotion and affect* (pp. 273–306). New York, NY: Raven Press.

Gray, J. A., & McNaughton, N. (2000). *The neuropsychology of anxiety: An enquiry into the functions of the septo-hippocampal system.* Oxford: Oxford University Press.

Greenaway, R. & Howlin, P. (2010). Dysfunctional attitudes and perfectionism and their relationship to anxious and depressive symptoms in boys with autism spectrum disorders. *Journal of Autism and Developmental Disorders, 40*(10), 1179–1187.

Grolnick, W. S., & Ryan, R. M. (1989). Parent styles associated with children's self-regulation and competence in school. *Journal of Educational Psychology, 81*(2), 143–154.

Grzegorek, J. L., Slaney, R. B., Franze, S., & Rice, K. G. (2004). Self-criticism, dependency, self-esteem, and grade point average satisfaction among clusters of perfectionists and nonperfectionists. *Journal of Counseling Psychology, 51*(2), 192–200.

Gurland, S. T., & Grolnick, W. S. (2005). Perceived threat, controlling parenting, and children's achievement orientations. *Motivation and Emotion, 29*(2), 103–121.

Haase, A. M., Prapavessis, H., & Owens, R. G. (2013). Domain-specificity in perfectionism: Variations across domains of life. *Personality and Individual Differences, 55*(6), 711–715.

Hall, H. K. (2016). Reflections on perfection and its influence on motivational processes in sports, dance, and exercise. In A. P. Hill (Ed), *The psychology of perfectionism in sport, dance and exercise* (pp. 275–295). New York, NY: Routledge/Taylor & Francis Group.

Hall, H. K., Kerr, A. W., & Matthews, J. (1998). Precompetitive anxiety in sport: The contribution of achievement goals and perfectionism. *Journal of Sport and Exercise Psychology, 20*(2), 194–217.

Hamachek, D. E. (1978). Psychodynamics of normal and neurotic perfectionism. *Psychology: A Journal of Human Behavior, 15*(1), 27–33.

Hanchon, T. A. (2010). The relations between perfectionism and achievement goals. *Personality and Individual Differences, 49*(8), 885–890.

Harackiewicz, J. M., Barron, K. E., Carter, S. M., Lehto, A. T., & Elliot, A. J. (1997). Predictors and consequences of achievement goals in the college classroom: Maintaining interest and making the grade. *Journal of Personality and Social Psychology, 73*(6), 1284–1295.

Harackiewicz, J. M., Barron, K. E., & Elliot, A. J. (1998). Rethinking achievement goals: When are they adaptive for college students and why? *Educational Psychologist, 33*(1), 1–21.

Harvey, B., Milyavskaya, M., Hope, N., Powers, T. A., Saffran, M., & Koestner, R. (2015). Affect variation across days of the week: Influences of perfectionism and academic motivation. *Motivation and Emotion, 39*(4), 521–530.

Hautzinger, M., Luka V., & Trautman R. D. (1986). Skala dysfunktionaler Einstellungen. Eine deutsche Version der Dysfunctional Attitude Scale. *Diagnostika, 31,* 312–323.

Hembree, R. (1988). Correlates, causes, effects, and treatment of test anxiety. *Review of Educational Research, 58*(1), 47–77.

Herman, K. C., Trotter, R., Reinke, W. M., & Ialongo, N. (2011). Developmental origins of perfectionism among African American youth. *Journal of Counseling Psychology, 58*(3), 321–334.

Herman, K. C., Wang, K., Trotter, R., Reinke, W. M., & Ialongo, N. (2013). Developmental trajectories of maladaptive perfectionism among African American adolescents. *Child Development, 84*(5), 1633–1650.

Hewitt, P. L., & Flett, G. L. (1991). Perfectionism in the self and social contexts: Conceptualization, assessment, and association with psychopathology. *Journal of Personality and Social Psychology, 60*(3), 456–470.

Hewitt, P. L., & Flett, G. L. (1993). Dimensions of perfectionism, daily stress, and depression: A test of the specific vulnerability hypothesis. *Journal of Abnormal Psychology, 102*(1), 58–65.

Hewitt, P. L., Flett, G. L., & Ediger, E. (1996). Perfectionism and depression: Longitudinal assessment of a specific vulnerability hypothesis. *Journal of Abnormal Psychology, 105*(2), 276–280.

Hewitt, P. L., Flett, G. L., & Mikail, S. F. (2017). *Perfectionism: A relational approach to conceptualization, assessment and treatment.* New York: Guilford Press.

Hewitt, P. L., Flett, G. L., Sherry, S. B., & Caelian, C. (2006). Trait perfectionism dimensions and suicidal behavior. In T. Ellis (Ed.), *Cognition and suicide: Theory, research, and therapy* (pp. 215–235). Washington, DC: American Psychological Association.

Hewitt, P. L., Flett, G. L., Sherry, S. B., Habke, M., Parkin, M., & Lam, R. W. (2003). The interpersonal expression of perfection: Perfectionistic self-presentation and psychological distress. *Journal of Personality and Social Psychology, 84*(6), 1303–1325.

Hibbard, D. R., & Walton, G. E. (2014). Exploring the development of perfectionism: The influence of parenting style and gender. *Social Behavior and Personality, 42*(2), 269–278.

Hill, A. P. (2014). Perfectionistic strivings and the perils of partialling. *International Journal of Sport and Exercise Psychology, 12*(4), 302–315.

Hill, A. P. (2016). *The psychology of perfectionism in sport, dance and exercise.* New York, NY: Routledge/Taylor & Francis Group.

Hill, A. P., & Curran, T. (2016). Multidimensional perfectionism and burnout: A meta-analysis. *Personality and Social Psychology Review, 20*(30), 269–288.

Hill, R. W., Huelsman, T. J., Furr, R. M., Kibler, J., Vicente, B. B., & Kennedy, C. (2004). A new measure of perfectionism: The Perfectionism Inventory. *Journal of Personality Assessment, 82*(1), 80–91.

Hodapp, V., Glanzmann, P. G., & Laux, L. (1995). Theory and measurement of test anxiety as a situation-specific trait. In C. D. Spielberger & P. R. Vagg (Eds.), *Test anxiety: Theory, assessment, and treatment* (pp. 47–58). Philadelphia, PA: Taylor & Francis.

Hong, R. Y., Lee, S. M., Chng, R. Y., Zhou, Y., Tsai, F., & Tan, S. H. (2016). Developmental trajectories of maladaptive perfectionism in middle childhood. *Journal of Personality.* doi:10.1111/jopy.12249

Hutchinson, A. J., & Yates, G. C. R. (2008). Maternal goal factors in adaptive and maladaptive childhood perfectionism. *Educational Psychology, 28*(7), 795–808.

Iranzo-Tatay, C., Gimeno-Clemente, N., Barberá-Fons, M., Ángeles Rodriguez-Campayo, M., Rojo-Bofill, L., Livianos-Aldana, L., Beato-Fernandez, L., Vaz-Leal, F., & Rojo-Moreno, L. (2015). Genetic and environmental contributions to perfectionism and its common factors. *Psychiatry Research, 230*(3), 932–939.

Jaradat, A.-K. M. (2013). Multidimensional perfectionism in a sample of Jordanian high school students. *Australian Journal of Guidance and Counseling, 23*(1), 95–105.

John, O. P., Naumann, L. P., & Soto, C. J. (2008). Paradigm shift to the integrative big-five trait taxonomy: History, measurement, and conceptual issues. In O. P. John, R. W. Robins, & L. A. Pervin (Eds.), *Handbook of personality: Theory and research* (pp. 114–158). New York, NY: Guilford Press.

Karavasilis, L., Doyle, A. B., & Markiewicz, D. (2003). Associations between parenting style and attachment to mother in middle childhood and adolescence. *International Journal of Behavioral Development, 27*(2), 153–164.

Kawamura, K. Y., Frost, R. O., & Harmatz, M. G. (2002). The relationship of perceived parenting styles to perfectionism. *Personality and Individual Differences, 32*(2), 317–327.

Kenney-Benson, G. A. & Pomerantz, E. M. (2005). The role of mothers' use of control in children's perfectionism: Implications for the development of children's depressive symptoms. *Journal of Personality, 73*(1), 23–46.

Khawaja, N. G., & Armstrong, K. A. (2005). Factor structure and psychometric properties of the Frost Multidimensional Perfectionism Scale: Developing shorter versions using an Australian sample. *Australian Journal of Psychology, 57*(2), 129–138.

Kim, B., Lee, M., Kim, K., Choi, H., & Lee, S. M. (2015). Longitudinal analysis of academic burnout in Korean middle school students. *Stress and Health: Journal of the International Society for the Investigation of Stress, 31*(4), 281–289.

Kim, K. R., & Seo, E. H. (2015). The relationship between procrastination and academic performance: A meta-analysis. *Personality and Individual Differences, 82*, 26–33.

Kopala-Sibley, D. C., & Zuroff, D. C. (2014). The developmental origins of personality factors from the self-definitional and relatedness domains: A review of theory and research. *Review of General Psychology, 18*(3), 137–155.

Kopala-Sibley, D. C., Zuroff, D. C., Hermanto, N., & Joyal-Desmarais, K. (2016). The development of self-definition and relatedness in emerging adulthood and their role in the development of depressive symptoms. *International Journal of Behavioral Development, 40*(4), 302–312.

Lee, J., Puig, A., Kim, Y., Shin, H., Lee, J. H., & Lee, S. M. (2010). Academic burnout profiles in Korean adolescents. *Stress and Health: Journal of the International Society for the Investigation of Stress, 26*(5), 404–416.

Lee, J., Puig, A., Lea, E., & Lee, S. M. (2013). Age-related differences in academic burnout of Korean adolescents. *Psychology in the Schools, 50*(10), 1015–1031.

Leonard, N. R., Gwadz, M. V., Ritchie, A., Linick, J. L., Cleland, C. M., Elliott, L., & Grethel, M. (2015). A multi-method exploratory study of stress, coping, and substance use among high school youth in private schools. *Frontiers in Psychology, 6*, 1028. doi:10.3389/fpsyg.2015.01028

Liebert, R. M., & Morris, L. W. (1967). Cognitive and emotional components of test anxiety: A distinction and some initial data. *Psychological Reports, 20*(3), 975–978.

Liew, J., Lench, H. C., Kao, G., Yeh, Y., & Kwok, O. (2014). Avoidance temperament and social-evaluative threat in college students' math performance: A mediation model of math and test anxiety. *Anxiety, Stress and Coping: An International Journal, 27*(6), 650–661.

Limburg, K., Watson, H. J., Hagger, M. S., & Egan, S. J. (2016). The relationship between perfectionism and psychopathology: A meta-analysis. *Journal of Clinical Psychology*. doi:10.1002/jclp.22435

Lyman, E. L., & Luthar, S. S. (2014). Further evidence on the 'costs of privilege': Perfectionism in high-achieving youth at socioeconomic extremes. *Psychology in the Schools, 51*(9), 913–930.

Maccoby, E. E., & Martin, J. A. (1983). Socialization in the context of the family: Parent-child interaction. In E. M. Hetherington (Ed.), *Handbook of child psychology: Vol. 4. Socialization, personality, and social development* (pp. 1–101). New York, NY: Wiley.

Madjar, N., Voltsis, M., & Weinstock, M. P. (2015). The roles of perceived parental expectation and criticism in adolescents' multidimensional perfectionism and achievement goals. *Educational Psychology, 35*(6), 765–778.

Martin, T. R., Flett, G. L., Hewitt, P. L., Krames, L., & Szantos, G. (1996). Personality correlates of depression and health symptoms: A test of a self-regulation model. *Journal of Research in Personality, 30*(2), 264–277.

Maslow, A. H. (1970). New introduction: Religions, values, and peak-experiences. *Journal of Transpersonal Psychology, 2*(2), 83–90.

May, R. W., Bauer, K. N., & Fincham, F. D. (2015). School burnout: Diminished academic and cognitive performance. *Learning and Individual Differences, 42*, 126–131.

MacCann, C., Duckworth, A. L., & Roberts, R. D. (2009). Empirical identification of the major facets of conscientiousness. *Learning and Individual Differences, 19*(4), 451–458.

McAbee, S. T., Oswald, F. L., & Connelly, B. S. (2014). Bifactor models of personality and college student performance: A broad versus narrow view. *European Journal of Personality, 28*(6), 604–619.

McArdle, S. (2010). Exploring domain-specific perfectionism. *Journal of Personality, 78*(2), 493–508.

McArdle, S., & Duda, J. L. (2004). Exploring social-contextual correlates of perfectionism in adolescents: A multivariate perspective. *Cognitive Therapy and Research, 28*(6), 765–788.

McArdle, S., & Duda, J. L. (2008). Exploring the etiology of perfectionism and perceptions of self-worth in young athletes. *Social Development, 17*(4), 980–997.

McCrae, R. R., & Costa, P. T. (1987). Validation of the five-factor model of personality across instruments and observers. *Journal of Personality and Social Psychology, 52*(1), 81–90.

Miller, A. L., Lambert, A. D., & Speirs Neumeister, K. L. (2012). Parenting style, perfectionism, and creativity in high-ability and high-achieving young adults. *Journal for the Education of the Gifted, 35*(4), 344–365.

Mills, J. S., & Blankstein, K. R. (2000). Perfectionism, intrinsic vs extrinsic motivation, and motivated strategies for learning: A multidimensional analysis of university students. *Personality and Individual Differences, 29*(6), 1191–1204.

Miquelon, P., Vallerand, R. J., Grouzet, F. E., & Cardinal, G. (2005). Perfectionism, academic motivation, and psychological adjustment: An integrative model. *Personality and Social Psychology Bulletin, 31*(7), 913–924.

Mitchell, J. H., Broeren, S., Newall, C., & Hudson, J. L. (2013). An experimental manipulation of maternal perfectionistic anxious rearing behaviors with anxious and non-anxious children. *Journal of Experimental Child Psychology*, *116*(1), 1–18.

Mitchelson, J. K., & Burns, L. R. (1998). Career mothers and perfectionism: Stress at work and at home. *Personality and Individual Differences*, *25*(3), 477–485.

Mobley, M., Slaney, R. S., & Rice, K. G. (2005). Construct validity and psychological and academic correlates of perfectionism among African-American college students. *Journal of Counseling Psychology*, *52*, 629–639.

Mounts, N. S., & Steinberg, L. (1995). An ecological analysis of peer influence on adolescent grade point average and drug use. *Developmental Psychology*, *31*(6), 915–922.

Mouratidis, A., Vansteenkiste, M., Lens, W., Michou, A., & Soenens, B. (2013). Within-person configurations and temporal relations of personal and perceived parent-promoted aspirations to school correlates among adolescents. *Journal of Educational Psychology*, *105*(3), 895–910.

National Research Council. (2004). *Engaging schools: Fostering high school students' motivation to learn*. Washington, DC: The National Academies Press.

Noftle, E. E., & Robins, R. W. (2007). Personality predictors of academic outcomes: Big Five correlates of GPA and SAT scores. *Journal of Personality and Social Psychology*, *93*(1), 116–130.

Nounopoulos, A., Ashby, J. S., & Gilman, R. (2006). Coping resources, perfectionism, and academic performance among adolescents. *Psychology in the Schools*, *43*(5), 613–622.

Novotney, A. (2014). Students under pressure. *Monitor on Psychology*, *45*(8), 36.

O'Connor, R. C., & Forgan, G. (2007). Suicidal thinking and perfectionism: The role of goal adjustment and behavioral inhibition/activation systems (BIS/BAS). *Journal of Rational-Emotive and Cognitive-Behavior Therapy*, *25*(4), 321–341.

Olson, D. H., Portner, J. & Bell, R. Q. (1982). *FACES II: Family adaptability and cohesion evaluation scales*. St. Paul: University of Minnesota, Family Social Science.

Onwuegbuzie, A. J. (2000). Academic procrastinators and perfectionistic tendencies among graduate students. *Journal of Social Behavior and Personality*, *15*(5), 103–109.

Ozer, B. U., O'Callaghan, J., Bokszczanin, A., Ederer, E., & Essau, C. (2014). Dynamic interplay of depression, perfectionism and self-regulation on procrastination. *British Journal of Guidance and Counseling*, *42*(3), 309–319.

Pacht, A. R. (1984). Reflections on perfection. *American Psychologist*, *39*(4), 386–390.

Padilla-Walker, L. M., & Nelson, L. J. (2012). Black hawk down?: Establishing helicopter parenting as a distinct construct from other forms of parental control during emerging adulthood. *Journal of Adolescence, 35*(5), 1177–1190.

Paunonen, S. V., & Ashton, M. C. (2013). On the prediction of academic performance with personality traits: A replication study. *Journal of Research in Personality, 47*(6), 778–781.

Pekrun, R. (2006). The control-value theory of achievement emotions: Assumptions, corollaries, and implications for educational research and practice. *Educational Psychology Review, 18*(4), 315–341.

Pekrun, R., Goetz, T., Titz, W., & Perry, R. P. (2002). Academic emotions in students' self-regulated learning and achievement: A program of qualitative and quantitative research. *Educational Psychologist, 37*(2), 91–105.

Pekrun, R., & Stephens, E. J. (2012). Academic emotions. In K. R. Harris, S. Graham, T. Urdan, J. M. Royer, & M. Zeidner (Eds.), *APA educational psychology handbook, Vol 2: Individual differences and cultural and contextual factors* (pp. 3–31). Washington, DC: American Psychological Association.

Perera, M. J., & Chang, E. C. (2015). Ethnic variations between Asian and European Americans in interpersonal sources of socially prescribed perfectionism: It's not just about parents! *Asian American Journal of Psychology, 6*(1), 31–37.

Pintrich, P. R., Smith, D. A., Garcia, T., & McKeachie, W. J. (1993). Reliability and predictive validity of the Motivated Strategies for Learning Questionnaire (MSLQ). *Educational and Psychological Measurement, 53*(3), 801–813.

Randles, D., Flett, G. L., Nash, K. A., McGregor, I. D., & Hewitt, P. L. (2010). Dimensions of perfectionism, behavioral inhibition, and rumination. *Personality and Individual Differences, 49*(2), 83–87.

Randolph, J. J., & Dykman, B. M. (1996). *Assessment of critical parenting experiences: The Critical Parenting Inventory.* 76th Annual Convention of the Western Psychological Association, San Jose, California.

Rasmussen, S. A., Elliott, M. A., & O'Connor, R. C. (2012). Psychological distress and perfectionism in recent suicide attempters: The role of behavioural inhibition and activation. *Personality and Individual Differences, 52*(6), 680–685.

Ratelle, C. F., Guay, F., Vallerand, R. J., Larose, S., & Senécal, C. (2007). Autonomous, controlled, and amotivated types of academic motivation: A person-oriented analysis. *Journal of Educational Psychology, 99*(4), 734–746.

Rice, K. G., Ashby, J. S., & Gilman, R. (2011). Classifying adolescent perfectionists. *Psychological Assessment, 23*(3), 563–577.

Rice, K. G., Ashby, J. S., & Preusser, K. J. (1996). Perfectionism, relationships with parents, and self-esteem. *Individual Psychology, 52*(3), 246–260.

Rice, K. G., Ashby, J. S., & Slaney, R. B. (2007). Perfectionism and the five-factor model of personality. *Assessment, 14*(4), 385–398.

Rice, K. G., & Dellwo, J. P. (2002). Perfectionism and self-development: Implications for college adjustment. *Journal of Counseling and Development, 80*(2), 188–196.

Rice, K. G., Leever, B. A., Christopher, J., & Porter, J. D. (2006). Perfectionism, stress, and social (dis)connection: A short-term study of hopelessness, depression, and academic adjustment among honors students. *Journal of Counseling Psychology, 53*(4), 524–534.

Rice, K. G., & Lopez, F. G. (2004). Maladaptive perfectionism, adult attachment, and self-esteem in college students. *Journal of College Counseling, 7*(2), 118–128.

Rice, K. G., Lopez, F. G., & Richardson, C. M. E. (2013). Perfectionism and performance among STEM students. *Journal of Vocational Behavior, 82*(2), 124–134.

Rice, K. G., Lopez, F. G., & Vergara, D. (2005). Parental/Social influences on perfectionism and adult attachment orientations. *Journal of Social and Clinical Psychology, 24*(4), 580–605.

Rice, K. G., & Mirzadeh, S. A. (2000). Perfectionism, attachment, and adjustment. *Journal of Counseling Psychology, 47*(2), 238–250.

Rice, K. G., Ray, M. E., Davis, D. E., DeBlaere, C., & Ashby, J. S. (2015). Perfectionism and longitudinal patterns of stress for STEM majors: Implications for academic performance. *Journal of Counseling Psychology, 62*(4), 718–731.

Rice, K. G., Richardson, C. M. E., & Clark, D. (2012). Perfectionism, procrastination, and psychological distress. *Journal of Counseling Psychology, 59*(2), 288–302.

Rice, K. G., Richardson, C. M. E., & Ray, M. E. (2016). Perfectionism in academic settings. In F. M. Sirois & D. S. Molnar (Eds.), *Perfectionism, health, and well-being* (pp. 245–264). Switzerland: Springer International Publishing.

Rice, K. G., & Slaney, R. B. (2002). Clusters of perfectionists: Two studies of emotional adjustment and academic achievement. *Measurement and Evaluation in Counseling and Development, 35*(1), 35–48.

Richardson, C. E., Rice, K. G., & Devine, D. P. (2014). Perfectionism, emotion regulation, and the cortisol stress response. *Journal of Counseling Psychology, 61*(1), 110–118.

Rikoon, S. H., Brenneman, M., Kim, L. E., Khorramdel, L., MacCann, C., Burrus, J., & Roberts, R. D. (2016). Facets of conscientiousness and their differential relationships with cognitive ability factors. *Journal of Research in Personality, 61*, 22–34.

Ryan, R. M., & Deci, E. L. (2002). Overview of self-determination theory: An organismic-dialectical perspective. In E. L. Deci, & R. M. Ryan (Eds.), *Handbook of self-determination research* (pp. 3–33). Rochester, NY: University of Rochester Press.

Salmela-Aro, K., Kiuru, N., & Nurmi, J. (2008). The role of educational track in adolescents' school burnout: A longitudinal study. *The British Psychological Society, 78*(4), 663–689.

Sapieja, K. M., Dunn, J. G. H., & Holt, N. L. (2011). Perfectionism and perceptions of parenting styles in male youth soccer. *Journal of Sport and Exercise Psychology, 33*(1), 20–39.

Sarason, I. G. (1984). Stress, anxiety, and cognitive interference: Reactions to tests. *Journal Of Personality and Social Psychology, 46*(4), 929–938.

Schaefer, E. S. (1965). Children's reports of parental behavior: An inventory. *Child Development, 36*(2), 413–424.

Schaufeli, W. B., Martínez, I. M., Marques Pinto, A., Salanova, M., & Bakker, A. B. (2002). Burnout and engagement in university students: A cross-national study. *Journal of Cross-Cultural Psychology, 33*(5), 464–481.

Schiffrin, H. H., Liss, M., Miles-McLean, H., Geary, K. A., Erchull, M. J., & Tashner, T. (2014). Helping or hovering? The effects of helicopter parenting on college students' well-being. *Journal of Child and Family Studies, 23*(3), 548–557.

Seipp, B. (1991). Anxiety and academic performance: A meta-analysis of findings. *Anxiety Research, 4*(1), 27–41.

Seo, E. H. (2008). Self-efficacy as a mediator in the relationship between self-oriented perfectionism and academic procrastination. *Social Behavior and Personality, 36*(6), 753–764.

Shafran, R., Cooper, Z., & Fairburn, C. G. (2002). Clinical perfectionism: A cognitive-behavioural analysis. *Behaviour Research and Therapy, 40*(7), 773–791.

Shafran, R., & Mansell, W. (2001). Perfectionism and psychopathology: A review of research and treatment. *Clinical Psychology Review, 21*(6), 879–906.

Shaunessy, E., Suldo, S. M., & Friedrich, A. (2011). Mean levels and correlates of perfectionism in International Baccalaureate and general education students. *High Ability Studies, 22*(1), 61–77.

Sherry, S. B., Gautreau, C. M., Mushquash, A. R., Sherry, D. L., & Allen, S. L. (2014). Self-critical perfectionism confers vulnerability to depression after controlling for neuroticism: A longitudinal study of middle-aged, community-dwelling women. *Personality and Individual Differences, 69*, 1–4.

Shih, S. S. (2012). An examination of academic burnout versus work engagement among Taiwanese adolescents. *The Journal of Educational Research, 105*(4), 286–298.

Shih, S. S. (2013). Autonomy support versus psychological control, perfectionism, and Taiwanese adolescents' achievement goals. *The Journal of Educational Research, 106*(4), 269–279.

Shih, S. (2015). An investigation into academic burnout among Taiwanese adolescents from the self-determination theory perspective. *Social Psychology of Education, 18*(1), 201–219.

Shim, S. S., Rubenstein, L. D., & Drapeau, C. W. (2016). When perfectionism is coupled with low achievement: The effects on academic engagement and help seeking in middle school. *Learning and Individual Differences, 45*, 237–244.

Siegle, D., & Schuler, P. A. (2000). Perfectionism differences in gifted middle school students. *Roeper Review, 23*(1), 39–45.

Simonds, J., & Rothbart, M. K. (2004, October). *The temperament in middle childhood questionnaire (TMCQ): A computerized self-reported measures of temperament for ages 7-10*. Poster session presented at the Occasional Temperament Conference, Athens, GA.

Simpson, J. A., Rholes, W. S., & Nelligan, J. S. (1992). Support-seeking and support-giving with couples in an anxiety-provoking situation: The role of attachment styles. *Journal of Personality and Social Psychology, 62*(3), 971–980.

Sirois, F. M. (2016). Perfectionism and health behaviors: A self-regulation resource perspective. In F. M. Sirois, & D. S. Molnar (Eds.), *Perfectionism, health, and well-being* (pp. 45–67). Cham, Switzerland: Springer International Publishing.

Sirois, F. M., & Kitner, R. (2015). Less adaptive or more maladaptive? A meta-analytic investigation of procrastination and coping. *European Journal of Personality, 29*(4), 433–444.

Sirois, F. M., & Molnar, D. S. (2016). *Perfectionism, health, and well-being*. Cham, Switzerland: Springer International Publishing.

Sirois, F. M., Molnar, D. M., & Hirsch, J. K. (in press). A meta-analytic and conceptual update on the associations between procrastination and multidimensional perfectionism. *European Journal of Personality*.

Slaney, R. B., & Johnson, D. G. (1992). *The Almost Perfect Scale*. Unpublished manuscript, Pennsylvania State University.

Slaney, R. B., Rice, K. G., Mobley, M., Trippi, J., & Ashby, J. S. (2001). The Revised Almost Perfect Scale. *Measurement and Evaluation in Counseling and Development, 34*(3), 130–145.

Soenens, B., Elliot, A. J., Goossens, L., Vansteenkiste, M., Luyten, P., & Duriez, B. (2005). The intergenerational transmission of perfectionism: Parents' psychological control as an intervening variable. *Journal of Family Psychology, 19*(3) 358–366.

Soenens, B., Luyckx, K., Vansteenkiste, M., Luyten, P., Duriez, B., & Goossens, L. (2008). Maladaptive perfectionism as an intervening variable between psychological control and adolescent depressive symptoms: A three-wave longitudinal study. *Journal of Family Psychology, 22*(3), 465–474.

Soenens, B., & Vansteenkiste, M. (2005). Antecedents and outcomes of self-determination in 3 life domains: The role of parents' and teachers' autonomy support. *Journal of Youth and Adolescence, 34*(6), 589–604.

Soenens, B., & Vansteenkiste, M. (2010). A theoretical upgrade of the concept of parental psychology control: Proposing new insights on the basis of self-determination theory. *Developmental Review, 30*(1), 74–99.

Soenens, B., Vansteenkiste, M., & Luyten, P. (2010). Toward a domain-specific approach to the study of parental psychological control: Distinguishing between dependency-oriented and achievement-oriented psychological control. *Journal of Personality, 78*(1), 217–256.

Solomon, L. J., & Rothblum, E. D. (1984). Academic procrastination: Frequency and cognitive-behavioral correlates. *Journal of Counseling Psychology, 31*(4), 503–509.

Soysa, C. K., & Weiss, A. (2014). Mediating perceived parenting styles-test anxiety relationships: Academic procrastination and maladaptive perfectionism. *Learning and Individual Differences, 34*, 77–85.

Speirs Neumeister, K. L. (2004). Factors influencing the development of perfectionism in gifted college students. *Gifted Child Quarterly, 48*(4), 259–274.

Speirs Neumeister, K. L. (2017). Perfectionism in gifted students. In J. Stoeber (Ed.), *The psychology of perfectionism: Theory, research, applications.* London: Routledge.

Speirs Neumeister, K. L., & Finch, W. H. (2006). Perfectionism in high-ability students: Relational precursors and implications for achievement. *Gifted Child Quarterly, 50*(3), 238–251.

Speirs Neumeister, K. L., Fletcher, K. L., & Burney, V. H. (2015). Perfectionism and achievement motivation in high-ability students: An examination of the 2 × 2 model of perfectionism. *Journal for the Education of the Gifted, 38*(3), 215–232.

Speirs Neumeister, K. L., Williams, K. K., & Cross, T. L. (2009). Gifted high-school students' perspectives on the development of perfectionism. *Roeper Review, 31*(4), 198–206.

Spence, J. T., & Helmreich, R. L. (1983). Beyond face validity: A comment on Nicholls, Licht, and Pearl. *Psychological Bulletin, 94*(1), 181–184.

Stoeber, J. (2011). The dual nature of perfectionism in sports: Relationships with emotion, motivation, and performance. *International Review of Sport and Exercise Psychology, 4*(2), 128–145.

Stoeber, J. (2014). Perfectionism in sport and dance: A double-edged sword. *International Journal of Sport Psychology, 45*(4), 385–394.

Stoeber, J. (2017). The psychology of perfectionism: Critical issues, open questions, and future directions. In J. Stoeber (Ed.), *The psychology of perfectionism: Theory, research, and applications*. London: Routledge.

Stoeber, J., & Corr, P. J. (2015). Perfectionism, personality, and affective experiences: New insights from revised Reinforcement Sensitivity Theory. *Personality and Individual Differences, 86*, 354–359.

Stoeber, J., Corr, P. J., Smith, M. M., & Saklofske, D. H. (2017). Perfectionism and personality. In J. Stoeber (Ed.), *The psychology of perfectionism: Theory, research, and applications*. London: Routledge.

Stoeber, J., & Damian, L. E. (2016). Perfectionism in employees: Work engagement, workaholism, and burnout. In F. M. Sirois & D. S. Molnar (Eds.), *Perfectionism, health, and well-being* (pp. 265–283). Cham, Switzerland: Springer International Publishing.

Stoeber, J., Damian, L. E., & Madigan, D. J. (2017). Perfectionism: A motivational perspective. In J. Stoeber (Ed.), *The psychology of perfectionism: Theory, research, and applications*. London: Routledge.

Stoeber, J., Feast, A. R., & Hayward, J. A. (2009). Self-oriented and socially prescribed perfectionism: Differential relationships with intrinsic and extrinsic motivation and test anxiety. *Personality and Individual Differences, 47*(5), 423–428.

Stoeber, J., & Gaudreau, P. (2017). The advantages of partialling perfectionistic strivings and perfectionistic concerns: Critical issues and recommendations. *Personality and Individual Differences, 104*, 379–386.

Stoeber, J., Haskew, A. E., & Scott, C. (2015). Perfectionism and exam performance: The mediating effect of task-approach goals. *Personality and Individual Differences, 74*, 171–176.

Stoeber, J., Hutchfield, J., & Wood, K. V. (2008). Perfectionism, self-efficacy, and aspiration level: Differential effects of perfectionistic striving and self-criticism after success and failure. *Personality and Individual Differences, 45*(4), 323–327.

Stoeber, J., Kempe, T., & Keogh, E. J. (2008). Facets of self-oriented and socially prescribed perfectionism and feelings of pride, shame, and guilt following success and failure. *Personality and Individual Differences, 44*(7), 1506–1516.

Stoeber, J., & Otto, K. (2006). Positive conceptions of perfectionism: Approaches, evidence, challenges. *Personality and Social Psychology Review, 10*(4), 295–319.

Stoeber, J., Otto, K., & Dalbert, C. (2009). Perfectionism and the Big Five: Conscientiousness predicts longitudinal increased in self-oriented perfectionism. *Personality and Individual Differences, 47*(4), 363–368.

Stoeber, J., Otto, K., & Stoll, O. (2006). *Multidimensional Inventory of Perfectionism* (MIPS): English version. Unpublished manuscript.

Stoeber, J., & Rambow, A. (2007). Perfectionism in adolescent school students: Relations with motivation, achievement, and well-being. *Personality and Individual Differences, 42*(7), 1379–1389.

Stoeber, J., & Stoeber, F. S. (2009). Domains of perfectionism: Prevalence and relationships with perfectionism, gender, age, and satisfaction with life. *Personality and Individual Differences, 46*(4), 530–535.

Stornelli, D., Flett, G. L. & Hewitt, P. L. (2009). Perfectionism, achievement, and affect in children: A comparison of students from gifted, arts, and regular programs. *Canadian Journal of School Psychology, 24*(4) 267–283.

Suddarth, B. H., & Slaney, R. G. (2001). An investigation of the dimensions of perfectionism in college students. *Measurement and Evaluation in Counseling and Development, 34*(3), 157–165.

Tong, Y., & Lam, S. F. (2011). The cost of being mother's ideal child: The role of internalization in the development of perfectionism and depression. *Social Development, 20*(3), 504–516.

Tozzi, F., Aggen, S. H., Neale, B. M., Anderson, C. B., Mazzeo, S. E., Neale, M. C., & Bulik, C. M. (2004). The structure of perfectionism: A twin study. *Behavior Genetics, 34*(5), 483–494.

Tuominen-Soini, H., & Salmela-Aro, K. (2013). Schoolwork engagement and burnout among Finnish high school students and young adults: Profiles, progressions, and educational outcomes. *Developmental Psychology, 50*(3), 649–662.

Turner, L. A., & Turner, P. E. (2011). The relation of behavioral inhibition and perceived parenting to maladaptive perfectionism in college students. *Personality and Individual Differences, 50*(6), 840–844.

Ulu, I. P., & Tezer, E. (2010). Adaptive and maladaptive perfectionism, adult attachment, and Big Five personality traits. *The Journal of Psychology, 144*(4), 327–340.

Usher, A., & Kober, N. (2012). *Student motivation: An overlooked piece of school reform*. Washington, DC: Center on Education Policy. Retrieved from www.cep-dc.org/displayDocument.cfm?DocumentID=405

Vallerand, R. J., Pelletier, L. G., Blais, M. R., Brière, N. M., Senecal, C., & Vallieres, E. F. (1993). On the assessment of intrinsic, extrinsic, and amotivation in education: Evidence on the concurrent and construct validity of the Academic Motivation Scale. *Educational and Psychological Measurement, 53*(1), 159–172.

van Beek, I., Kranenburg, I. C., Taris, T. W., & Schaufeli, W. B. (2013). BIS- and BAS-activation and study outcomes: A mediation study. *Personality and Individual Differences, 55*(5), 474–479.

Vansteenkiste, M., Smeets, S., Soenens, B., Lens, W., Matos, L., & Deci, E. L. (2010). Autonomous and controlled regulation of performance-approach goals: Their relations to perfectionism and educational outcomes. *Motivation and Emotion, 34*(4), 333–353.

Van Yperen, N. W. (2006). A novel approach to assessing achievement goals in the context of the 2×2 framework: Identifying distinct profiles of individuals with different dominant achievement goals. *Personality and Social Psychology Bulletin, 32*(11), 1432–1445.

Vergauwe, J., Wille, B., Feys, M., De Fruyt, F., & Anseel, F. (2015). Fear of being exposed: The trait-relatedness of the impostor phenomenon and its relevance in the work context. *Journal of Business and Psychology, 30*(3), 565–581.

Verner-Filion, J., & Gaudreau, P. (2010). From perfectionism to academic adjustment: The mediating role of achievement goals. *Personality and Individual Differences, 49*(3), 181–186.

Vieth, A. Z., & Trull, T. J. (1999). Family patterns of perfectionism: An examination of college students and their parents. *Journal of Personality Assessment, 72*(1), 49–67.

Walburg, V. (2014). Burnout among high school students: A literature review. *Children and Youth Services Review, 42*, 28–33.

Wang, K. T. (2012). Personal and family perfectionism of Taiwanese college students: Relationships with depression, self-esteem, achievement motivation, and academic grades. *International Journal of Psychology, 47*(4), 305–314.

Wang, K. T., Fu, C., & Rice, K. G. (2012). Perfectionism in gifted students: Moderating effects of goal orientation and contingent self-worth. *School Psychology Quarterly, 27*(2), 96–108.

Wei, M., Heppner, P. P., Russell, D. W., & Young, S. K. (2006). Maladaptive perfectionism and ineffective coping as mediators between attachment and future depression: A prospective analysis. *Journal of Counseling Psychology, 53*(1), 67–79.

Wei, M., Mallinckrodt, B., Russell, D. W., & Abraham, W. T. (2004). Maladaptive perfectionism as a mediator and moderator between adult attachment and depressive mood. *Journal of Counseling Psychology, 51*(2), 201–212.

Weiner, B. A., & Carton, J. S. (2012). Avoidant coping: A mediator of maladaptive perfectionism and test anxiety. *Personality and Individual Differences, 52*(5), 632–636.

Weissman, A. N., & Beck, A. T. (1978, November). *Development and validation of the Dysfunctional Attitude Scale: A preliminary investigation.* Paper presented at the meeting for the Association for the Advancement of Behavioral Therapy, Chicago.

Wentzel, K. R. (2009). Students' relationships with teachers as motivational contexts. In K. R. Wenzel & A. Wigfield (Eds.), *Handbook of motivation at school* (pp. 301–322). New York, NY: Routledge/Taylor & Francis Group.

Witcher, L. A., Alexander, E. S., Onwuegbuzie, A. J., Collins, K. M. T., & Witcher, A. E. (2007). The relationship between psychology students' levels of perfectionism and achievement in a graduate-level research methodology course. *Personality and Individual Differences, 43*(6), 1396–1405.

Yang, H., Guo, W., Yu, S., Chen, L., Zhang, H., Pan, L., & Wang, C. (2016). Personal and family perfectionism in Chinese school students: Relationships with learning stress, learning satisfaction and self-reported academic performance level. *Journal of Child and Family Studies, 25*(12), 3675–3683.

Zeidner, M. (1998). *Test anxiety: The state of the art.* New York, NY: Plenum Press.

Zeidner, M., & Matthews, G. (2005). Evaluation anxiety: Current theory and research. In A. J. Elliot & C. S. Dweck (Eds.), *Handbook of competence and motivation* (pp. 141–163). New York, NY: Guilford Publications.

Zhang, Y., Gan, Y., & Cham, H. (2007). Perfectionism, academic burnout and engagement among Chinese college students: A structural equation modeling analysis. *Personality and Individual Differences, 43*(6), 1529–1540.

Index

TITLES FROM OUR PSYCHOLOGY COLLECTION

Justice in Life and Society: How We Decide What is Fair
by Virginia Murphy-Berman

A Guide for Statistics in the Behavioral Sciences
by Jeff Foster

*College Student Psychological Adjustment: Exploring Relational
Dynamics that Predict Success*
by Jonathan F. Mattanah

*College Student Psychological Adjustment:
Theory, Methods, and Statistical Trends*
by Jonathan F. Mattanah

Momentum Press is one of the leading book publishers in the field of engineering,
mathematics, health, and applied sciences. Momentum Press offers over 30 collections,
including Aerospace, Biomedical, Civil, Environmental, Nanomaterials, Geotechnical,
and many others.

Momentum Press is actively seeking collection editors as well as authors. For more
information about becoming an MP author or collection editor, please visit
http://www.momentumpress.net/contact

Announcing Digital Content Crafted by Librarians

Momentum Press offers digital content as authoritative treatments of advanced engineering top-
ics by leaders in their field. Hosted on ebrary, MP provides practitioners, researchers, faculty,
and students in engineering, science, and industry with innovative electronic content in sensors
and controls engineering, advanced energy engineering, manufacturing, and materials science.

Momentum Press offers library-friendly terms:

- perpetual access for a one-time fee
- no subscriptions or access fees required
- unlimited concurrent usage permitted
- downloadable PDFs provided
- free MARC records included
- free trials

The **Momentum Press** digital library is very affordable, with no obligation to buy in future years.

For more information, please visit **www.momentumpress.net/library** or to set up a trial in the US,
please contact **mpsales@globalepress.com**.

www.ingramcontent.com/pod-product-compliance
Lightning Source LLC
Chambersburg PA
CBHW05071828 0326
41926CB00088B/3196